ASBESTOS IN THE SCHOOLS

ASBESTOS IN THE SCHOOLS

A Guide For School Administrators, Teachers and Parents

Carolyn Harvey and Mark Rollinson

PRAEGER

New York
Westport, Connecticut
London

Library of Congress Cataloging-in-Publication Data

Harvey, Carolyn.
    Asbestos in the schools: a guide for school administrators,
teachers, and parents/Carolyn Harvey and Mark Rollinson.
    p.   cm.
    Bibliography: p.
    Includes index.
    ISBN 0-275-92852-7 (alk. paper)
    1. Asbestos in building—United States—Safety measures.
2. School buildings—United States—Safety measures. 3. School
children—Health and hygiene—United States. I. Rollinson, Mark.
II. Title.
TA455.A6H37 1987   87-22888
363.1'79—dc19   CIP

Library of Congress Catalog Card Number: 87-22888
ISBN: 0-275-92852-7

First published in 1987

Praeger Publishers, One Madison Avenue, New York, NY 10010
A division of Greenwood Press, Inc.

Printed in the United States of America

∞™

The paper used in this book complies with the Permanent
Paper Standard issued by the National Information Standards
Organization (Z39.48-1984).

10 9 8 7 6 5 4 3 2 1

Table of Contents

Preface

For several years, school managements have been faced with some agonizing decisions. The crisis continues to heighten.

On the one hand there loom specters of personal criminal and civil liability for having failed to abate asbestos hazards in the past, for failing to do so in the present, and for doing so improperly in the future.

On the other hand there are the haunting truths that investors in the asbestos industry (encouraged and subsidized by government until only recently) are facing economic destruction, that under the worst circumstances even the theoretical risks to students from school exposure to asbestos are a small fraction of the risks of being killed in a school bus or being hit by lightning, and that there are dramatically better uses for the scarce resources that will be needed to abate asbestos.

The purpose of this book is to summarize the available knowledge pertinent to the decisions that school administrators, school board members, parents, and advisers must make in coming months and years.

Introduction

What we know today as "asbestosis" appears to have been known to the Babylonians. We long have known of cuneiform records of breathing problems in asbestos miners. The Romans, who used asbestos for draperies, linings of funeral pyres, and implements for handling hot tools, appear also to have been aware of lung problems developing in persons who mined asbestos.

Asbestos appears not to have been used to any significant extent, in Europe at least, from the fall of the Roman Empire until the Renaissance. From then until World War II its use gradually increased in all commercially important countries.

The United States has not been a major source of asbestos. As the mineral increased in commercial importance, the lack of domestic sources came to be of great concern. As early as 1921, legislation was enacted to stimulate domestic exploration and production. From World War II until the early 1970s, the domestic industry was encouraged and subsidized. As late as 1973 *United States Mineral Resources*, an official publication of the U.S. government, contained expression of concern over U.S. dependence on foreign sources for this important substance.

Modern concern over possible health hazards associated with asbestos is generally believed to have begun in Great Britain in 1906. By the 1930s there existed a respectable data base in Europe and the United States regarding a statistically significant connection between breathing asbestos fiber on the one hand and contracting asbestosis, lung cancer, and a rare and terrible form of cancer called mesothelioma on the other hand.

These risks seemed well worth taking. No other substance was (or is) known that provides such stability, strength, and heat resistance so efficiently. At its peak, asbestos was found in over 2,500 products. It is estimated that the use of asbestos has saved hundreds of thousands of lives, possibly millions, from the ravages of fire. In the 1950s and 1960s, in every state of the union, building codes specified asbestos as a required building material for at least some applications. It is little wonder that the United States was so concerned about foreign dependence.

Suddenly, in the middle 1970s, primarily as a result of court decisions, the climate changed. What only recently was regarded as one of the most beneficial substances known to man became a hazardous curse. The impact of the change is just beginning to be felt. While at this writing a staggering some 50,000 asbestos-related suits have been brought, it is estimated that the number will rise to nearly 200,000 by 2010.

The legal reaction occurred at least in part because of the discovery of evidence of cover-up in the 1920s and 1930s by U.S. industry officials. Industry officials protest that the incriminating correspondence is forged and contrived. Whether it is or not, the legal climate in which it allegedly was written was much different than it is today. These papers were arguably humane and normal several decades ago. Today they seem brutally callous to what is generally perceived as every person's right to a totally safe environment.

Law does not operate in a vacuum and serves no useful purpose in and of itself. Law is useful only to the extent that it provides a stable yet flexible environment in which one can perform useful tasks. Ideally that environment offers enough order to be predictable but is sufficiently open to permit creativity and progress. While it has seemed to us to be a shame that our society operates under such complex rules that the services of legal counsel are required for even the simplest matters, it is equally unfair that one cannot achieve a reasonable degree of predictability even with the assistance of legal counsel and that conduct that is acceptable one day may be judged by a new and different standard in the future.

Now, in addition to lawyers, we seem also to need statisticians, scientists, and, to be safe, soothsayers as well. Business entities that are roughly 40 percent owned by pension funds and an additional 40 percent by small investors (either directly or through mutual funds) are being pushed to bankruptcy for having failed, under ex post facto rules, to meet standards unheard of under prior patterns of conduct.

The legal and scientific confusion surrounding asbestos appears to be an example of society operating to its own detriment. Although one of the authors is a principal beneficiary of the confusion (being in the asbestos abatement business), the whole thing is bewildering. It occurred to us that others may be confused as well, particularly persons involved with schools who must make some momentous decisions in coming years. Hence this book.

One of the authors is a physical scientist by training and an environmental engineer by experience, with credentials as a person dedicated to a clean environment that have never been questioned and with professional involvement in abatement of a great variety of truly hazardous substances.

The other author is a business lawyer of considerable experience who has never litigated on either side of an asbestos case. We both have talked to many lawyers involved in asbestos litigation and have come to believe that the whole process is unproductive to the point of being shamelessly wasteful. But that is of little help to people who have to make difficult institutional decisions, frequently with limited budgets, and difficult personal decisions as well.

Schools will have to make many agonizing decisions in 1987 and in coming years. Prior to August 1, 1987, for instance, every primary and secondary school in the United States, public and private, must have decided whether to participate in the class action suit now going on in federal court in the Eastern District of Pennsylvania. Over coming months, possibly years, additional questions must be answered. How much asbestos do we have in our school? When should it be removed? How will we finance the removal? What should we tell parents and students in the meantime? What should we do about asbestos substitutes that are showing workplace harm similar to that of asbestos?

In addition to these questions that cannot be avoided, there are some questions that probably should be considered, such as the following: How can we benefit from this experience? How can we help future generations avoid similar predicaments? After all, if schools will not undertake these educational tasks, who will?

This book answers none of the foregoing questions. However, it does attempt to give, in a dispassionate way, a great deal of information that we hope will be useful to those attempting to forge intelligent answers.

ASBESTOS IN THE SCHOOLS

ONE
HISTORICAL PERSPECTIVE

This chapter is divided into three sections having to do with "asbestos," "words," and "numbers." Understanding each section is important to understanding the rest of this book. In addition, we think the reader will find these sections to be interesting and thought-provoking.

ASBESTOS

Asbestos has been used at least from the beginning of recorded history. The Egyptians used asbestos as embalming cloth; the Romans used it for cremation wrappings and for everlasting wicks in the lamps of the Vestal Virgins. Charlemagne used an asbestos tablecloth that was cleaned after feasts by tossing it into the flames of a fireplace. Marco Polo reported that asbestos clothing was used in China. In 1647 a physician named de Boot gave a recipe for a "miraculous asbestos ointment" for curing infectious skin diseases (which recipe also included lead, zinc, and calcinate).

Not until the nineteenth century, however, did asbestos come into widespread use. Its popularity mushroomed for roughly 100 years. In 1968 the United States consumed 817,000 tons of asbestos. In 1973 it was estimated that by the year 2000 domestic consumption would reach some 1,800,000 tons each year. That now appears unlikely, however. By 1982 domestic consumption had declined to 247,000 tons. On the other hand, consumption of other asbestiform fibers had risen dramatically. By 1977, for example, domestic consumption of fibrous glass had reached some 1,500,000 tons. By 1981 Attapulgite consumption had reached 712,000 tons. Other natural and man-made asbestiform substances have been, and are, making great strides.

Asbestos still is used for many things, of necessity, although increasing numbers of applications are being banned.

Like the use of asbestos, the occupational health hazards associated with excessive breathing of asbestos fibers over long periods have been documented since the very earliest days of recorded history. In modern times, scientific observation seems to have begun in the Western world in the 1800s and governments began to take notice in the early 1900s. In Europe, especially in England, medical and governmental authorities began recording serious pulmonary illnesses and deaths occurring in asbestos factory and mill workers at the turn of the century.

In North America concerns over asbestos-related occupational health hazards began being expressed about a decade later, first in Canada, then in the United States. In a 1918 bulletin titled *Mortality from Respiratory Diseases in Dusty Trades*, issued by the U.S. Bureau of Labor Statistics, there was reported "the practice of American and Canadian insurance companies not to insure asbestos workers due to their assumed health risks."

The year 1924 is considered by some to be a milestone in occupational health hazards from asbestos as a result of the widespread circulation of an article in the *British Medical Journal* entitled "Fibrosis of the Lungs due to the Inhalation of Asbestos Dust." Subsequent open discussion of the problem led Parliament in 1930 to promulgate environmental regulations regarding asbestos.

In 1938 proposed guidelines for acceptable asbestos dust concentrations in the workplace were published by the U.S. Public Health Service, possibly motivated by 1935 reports of lung cancer associated with long breathing of excessive quantities of asbestos.

Scholarly study of asbestos in the workplace continued from the 1930s to recent times. During the latter part of the 1960s concern arose over the widespread release of asbestos fibers into the air around construction sites. Public agencies at the municipal and state levels began to respond to the awareness that the use of asbestos-containing spray-on coatings represented a possible environmental hazard and a hazard to the workmen applying the materials. Boston, New York, Philadelphia, and Illinois banned the use of sprayed asbestos in 1970 and 1971.

Meanwhile, in the 1970 edition of *United States Mineral Resources*, an official publication of the U.S. government, May and Lewis, noted:

Medical problems connected with asbestos have been under intense study in recent years and undoubtedly will continue to warrant increasing attention in the future. In addition to study and medical treatment of the effects of asbestos on the respiratory system, work should be aimed at improved methods of protecting workers in mines, mills, and fabricating plants. Among the possibilities for solving the problems, in addition to medical study and treatment, are much greater use of automation where feasible, remote control of fabrication processes, improved protective equipment and respiratory devices, and development and strict enforcement of safety procedures.

In the same book, however, on the same page, it was noted that one of the most serious problems confronting the domestic consuming industry is our dependence for the greater part of our supply of asbestos on foreign sources. The article goes on to call for strategic stockpiling of asbestos and notes with approval work then under way aimed at developing even larger-scale asbestos uses.

While the above article was being written, some dramatic developments were plodding through U.S. courts. What is generally regarded as the seminal case, *Borel* v. *Fibreboard Paper Products Corp.*, reached the federal court of appeals in 1973. Borel was exposed to asbestos on the job from 1936 to 1969, when he became disabled with asbestosis and, a year later, mesothelioma. The facts and issues in his successful action typify those in personal injury asbestos litigation in general. Those issues are well known and will not be repeated here. However, one or two are interesting and worthy of note.

Counsel to the asbestos industry have taken two unusual positions that some lawyers, perhaps with the benefit of hindsight, consider to have been unfortunate. First, they have pleaded (and still plead) ignorance of the hazards involved, and hence inability to give warning. Second, they have refused (except in a case in Hawaii and possibly a few others) to raise the defense that many uses of asbestos were mandated by government building codes or procurement specifications or both. The reasons fly in the face of common sense and are illustrative, in our view, of hyperlegal mentalities obfuscating the real issues.

The plea of ignorance was made in fear. But it was impossible to prove because the risks were quite generally known. Even the asbestos industry itself had begun to respond to changing social attitudes toward risk. In 1964 warnings began to appear on asbestos products to the effect that inhalation of asbestos in excessive quantities over long periods of time may be harmful and that workers should avoid breathing asbestos dust. (The *Borel* court considered these admonitions to be inadequate, so much so as to constitute "black humor," in the judge's opinion.) Johns-Manville in 1969 adopted a policy of not selling asbestos fiber for nonessential uses that might unduly expose the general public—for example, modeling compounds used in grade schools.

To our "Monday morning quarterback" minds, under these circumstances a 1970 plea much more plausible than ignorance would have been that the risks were so generally known for such a long time that warning would have been as absurd as being obliged to warn a coal miner that he might get black lung or an automobile driver that he might have an accident. One additional irony of the industry position on ignorance has been the effect of extending the statute of limitations in many instances.

Refusal to raise the defense of government mandate has been founded, we are told by knowledgeable persons, on the belief that industry salespeople lobbied hard to obtain the building codes and regulations. It is easy to prove, however, that essentially all government standards are the result of someone's lobbying. People who make durable bottle cases lobby against disposable bottles under the banners of beauty and saving natural resources. Domestic manufacturers of bicycles lobby for bulky safety devices applied in the factory, under the flag of safety (but in reality to increase costs for foreign manufacturers). Most government regulators would deny vehemently that they routinely are influenced in this fashion. And most juries probably would believe them.

In any event, an unparalleled situation in U.S. tort law began to unfold about 1970 and other branches of government have reacted swiftly and decisively.

Spraying asbestos for fireproofing and insulation purposes was banned by the Environmental Protection Agency (EPA) in 1973. It later became apparent that the regulations were not sufficiently broad because they banned only insulation and fireproofing applications and not decorative uses, a perceived defect that was cured by regulation in 1978.

One of the early state actions specifically directed toward schools was the New York State School Asbestos Safety Act of 1979. The act gives broad permissive authority to the state commissioner of education to set standards and the like, and requires local school authorities to inspect and report to the commissioner on asbestos materials in schools, to develop a plan for the containment or removal of hazardous asbestos materials, to estimate the cost thereof, and to require contractors and supervisory personnel engaged in the containment or removal to have received adequate training. The act does not require removal.

Other states have passed similar legislation — for example, New Jersey in 1984. At this writing 32 states have enacted more than 60 asbestos-related laws, three-fourths of them passed in 1985 and 1986.

Congress acted with the Asbestos School Hazard Detection and Control Act of 1980, which required various studies and inspection and authorized financial assistance to schools. No funds were ever appropriated, however. The Department of Education estimated the cost of abatement, based upon reports received from the states, to be $1.4 billion. In a later report prepared by the EPA (but never published), the cost estimate for schools was doubled. As noted in Chapter 4, removal costs vary greatly. However, it is our opinion that a more accurate estimate of cost is more on the order of $400 billion and that the EPA internal report was never published because the cost methodology is suspect and because even the defective numbers are too inflammatory to be circulated.

In May 1982 the EPA published the "Asbestos-in-Schools" rule, which, among other things, required schools to identify friable asbestos, test the air, and notify employees and parent-teacher groups of the findings. A deadline of June 28, 1983, was mandated. As of the end of 1986, according to EPA regional coordinators, 60 percent of U.S. schools had failed to comply with the regulation.

Congress acted again with the Asbestos School Hazard Abatement Act (ASHAA) of 1984, which transferred authority for overseeing removal matters from the Department of Education to the EPA (a great political victory for the latter agency). This act again authorized grant and loan funding to assist with abatement. Some $50 million was appropriated in 1984, 1985, and 1986, even though the EPA requested no funds.

Meanwhile, the EPA supplemented its 1973 ban on sprayed product in 1979 with its publication of *Asbestos-Containing Materials in School Buildings: A Guidance Document.* Then, in January 1986, the agency proposed sweeping regulations to prohibit the manufacture, importation, and processing of asbestos in certain products and to phase out the use of asbestos in all other products except a handful that might come to be permitted under a stringent exemption process. This proposed rule, which still is pending, would immediately ban asbestos cement pipe and fittings, roofing felts, flooring felts, vinyl-asbestos floor tile, and asbestos clothing. Asbestos friction products (such as brake linings) would be prohibited after five years and all other products at a still later date. In the meantime, products not yet banned would be required to bear frightful labels.

In August 1986 the EPA, discouraged over non-compliance with its 1982 directive to schools, published for comment a proposed rule on a program for more aggressive enforcement of existing regulations regarding asbestos in schools and for promulgation of additional school regulations under the Toxic Substances Control Act (TSCA).

Congress put teeth in the proposed rule and expanded upon it with the enactment of the Asbestos Hazard Emergency Response Act (AHERA) of 1986, analyzed in great detail in Appendix A. Under this act, abatement is mandated for all friable school asbestos and some nonfriable. Brightly colored, large-type labels are to be placed on certain asbestos awaiting abatement. The EPA is required to make and enforce more stringent regulations relating to asbestos.

The EPA's response to the AHERA was to hold an open meeting on December 8, 1986, to discuss strategies for response to the act and to form an advisory committee and a negotiating process under which representatives of all interested classes can participate in the rulemaking mandated by Congress under the act. The proposed rule is set forth in full in Appendix B. It is expected to become final in October 1987.

The rule adopted will have great impact on schools. The financial impact will be many billions of dollars.

THE WORDS WE USE

The following may appear at first glance to be another boring glossary. It is not. It is a brief and, we hope, interesting essay on the use and misuse of words in connection with asbestos.

The term "asbestos" is a generic term applied to a wide chemical range of naturally occurring mineral silicates that separate into fibers. Their composition varies widely. Some have so much iron that they cannot be used for electrical insulation. Some contain magnesium, sodium, calcium, or a combination thereof.

The term "asbestiform" is useful for describing a variety of natural and manmade substances whose physical properties are essentially the same as asbestos. Such natural mineral fibers other than asbestos are legion. The most important commercially are palygorskite (commercially known as Attapulgite) and sepiolite, the commercial term for an assortment of minerals including meerschaum, which makes valuable pipes for tobacco smoking.

The synthetic asbestiform fibers include mineral wool, carbon fibers, ceramic fibers, and, most important by tonnage, fibrous glass.

Urban-dwelling humans are exposed in varying degrees to breathing all of the foregoing, and everyone is exposed to the natural asbestiform fibers that reach the air due to weathering and human disturbance of deposits.

Frequently we read of "friable" (pronounced and sometimes spelled "fryable") asbestos. The word entered the English language in the late 1500s and comes from the Latin verb *friare* meaning "to crumble into small pieces." According to the *Oxford English Dictionary*, the correct English meaning is "capable of being easily crumbled or reduced to powder." Sometimes in modern usage "easily" is defined as "by hand." Strictly speaking, it is not the asbestos that is friable (although asbestos does erode easily with wind and rain) but the material in which it is encapsulated. Thus a spray-on ceiling that crumbles easily on physical contact is correctly said to be a "friable" substance and, if asbestos fibers are released into the air, is then popularly called "friable asbestos." Very small amounts of asbestos can be released into the air from wear or damage to harder substances, such as vinyl asbestos floor tile. The fibers so released sometimes incorrectly are called "friable asbestos." In this book the term "friable" is used only correctly.

In 1927 an Englishman named Cooke coined the term "asbestosis" for nonmalignant pulmonary fibrosis (lung scarring) contracted by workers exposed to breathing high levels of asbestos fibers over extended periods.

Mesothelioma is a diffuse cancer, first reported in 1870, that spreads over either the surface of the lungs (pleural mesothelioma) or over the surface of the stomach lining (peritoneal mesothelioma).

Both kinds usually are marked by severe pain that in many cases is unresponsive to analgesics. Death usually occurs 3 to 24 months from the date of diagnosis. It is a rare form of cancer, now known to be induced, if not caused, principally but not exclusively by exposure to asbestos fibers.

Lung cancer other than pleural mesothelioma, peritoneal mesothelioma, and pulmonary fibrosis all have been linked to breathing asbestos fibers. All, of course, also have been linked to other phenomena.

The transitive form of the verb "cause" means "to be the cause of," "to bring about," "to make happen," "to effect," "to induce," or "to produce." The word in normal usage has both an air of absolutism and an air of proximity. That is, if ingestion of large quantities of arsenic is said to "cause" death in humans, the inference is that in all save the most extraordinary cases it absolutely will do so and there can be said to be no other phenomenon (such as having a head cold at the time of ingestion) that may be said to be the proximate cause of the individual's demise.

In casual usage, particularly in popular writing about environmental and health matters, the word "cause" frequently is used when what it meant is "making more susceptible" or some similar concept. Thus, though the surgeon general warns us from billboards throughout the land that "cigarette smoking causes cancer," that clearly is not the case, else all who smoke would contract the disease. What the statement should be, in a general way, is "If you have a genetic predisposition to contract lung cancer due, probably, to a deficient immune system, and you come to be under severe stress, there is a high probability that you will contract lung cancer from any one of a number of facilitating sources, one of the principal ones of which is cigarette smoking."

In this book the word "cause" is limited to its precise meaning.

The term "carcinogen" means "a substance that causes cancer." In popular usage, however, the word sometimes is used to mean a substance the exposure to which appears to be statistically associated with a higher rate of affliction with cancer than is experienced by the population at large. The cause of cancer appears not to be known at this time. The most promising present theories are that cancer is caused by a breakdown in the immune system of persons with defective immune systems. Since the cause of cancer is unknown and since there may be no substance that causes cancer, we have adopted the popular meaning of the word "carcinogen" rather than the correct use.

The word "abatement" has several meanings but a sense of reduction, diminution, decrease, or mitigation is present in many of the uses, and a concept of pulling down or putting an end to a matter is present in the rest. "Abatement" is used in the asbestos business in both senses. That is, "abatement" can refer to encapsulation of asbestos in place or it can refer to outright removal.

The term "risk" means "a chance of injury, damage or loss." Unfortunately, the term conveys no sense of magnitude of chance. Thus, if one were to walk through a minefield during a thunderstorm, one would risk being blown to smithereens and one would risk being hit by lightning. The degree of risk of each hazard would be quite different, yet the same word, "risk," is applied to each.

In common parlance, the term "risk" tends to connote something that is more likely than not. In this book the term is applied to chances however likely or remote, there being no other word of which we are aware that conveys the concept of the full spectrum of chance of undesirable consequences.

Closely related to risk is the word "hazard." "Hazard" tends to convey a sense of imminent danger and a likelihood greater than mere risk. Thus, a "hazardous waste" would be regarded by most as having a higher probability of undesirable consequences than would a "risky waste." However, neither "hazard" nor "risk" conveys a quantified concept.

THE NUMBERS WE USE

Whenever one deals with things "hazardous," one must understand the concept of risk, which in turn involves understanding probabilities, costs, and tangible and intangible benefits. These matters frequently require an understanding of very difficult mathematical concepts and the significance of very large and very small numbers. Unfortunately, these matters are beyond the easy grasp of most of us and can be appreciated only after painstakingly careful thought. Sometimes even the basics seem to escape many of us.

On the quiz show "Jeopardy" recently, a contestant was given an opportunity near the end of the game to bring himself to a winning position if he could calculate 30 percent of 30. His answer, obviously a guess, was "eight." This college-educated adult, who had been able to recall astoundingly obscure authors, plays, geographic trivia, popular songs, and names of creatures from the animal kingdom, was incapable of multiplying three times three!

It seems always to have been true that the population at large in a general way has been more advanced in linguistic skills than in mathematical skills. Historically, however, there has been a valid correlation between the extent of general mathematical skills and the material well-being of a civilization.

A magnificent example of the games one can play with statistical associations is the observation that in a general way societal sophistication in mathematics is directly proportionate to societal use of asbestos! Mathematics as an organized, independent, and reasoned discipline did not exist before the Greeks of the period from 600 to 300 B.C., people who used asbestos. There were, however, prior civilizations in which the beginnings or rudiments of mathematics were created, those of the Babylonians and Egyptians of about 3000 B.C., both early users of asbestos.

The correlation suggested is nonsense, of course, but it is interesting to note how slowly the most elementary mathematics made its first steps. In his marvelous book, *Mathematical Thought from Ancient to Modern Times,* Morris Kline summarizes the tedious advances in mathematical development. Though he does not make the historical point, Kline's work makes it clear that while many civilizations have built, plowed, manufactured, organized governments, and worshiped, invariably those with advanced mathematical skills came to dominate those less inclined to mathematical discipline. This distinction can be traced from the earliest times to modern civilization.

Perhaps the simplest (and least controversial) example is found in the Babylonians, who dominated their neighbors. They used their knowledge of arithmetic and simple algebra to express lengths and weights, to exchange money and merchandise, to compute simple and compound interest, to calculate taxes, to apportion shares of a harvest among farmer, church, and state, to divide inheritances, and to calculate work required for projects.

While the science of mathematics has advanced tremendously, and is an integral part of all important fields of study, the population at large today is still far behind—an example pertinent to the subject of this book—even those of us with a reasonable mastery of numbers have great difficulty with (a) very large and very small numbers and (b) with the significance of more than two or three digits.

It never ceases to amaze us, for example, how often one sees numbers like $11,842.19 in a long-term business plan. Most people would have difficulty comprehending (much less predicting) the differences among 10, 11, and 12. A few geniuses might be able to think clearly about the differences among 117, 118, and 119. And a still smaller group may be able to make meaningful thought distinctions among 1,183, 1,184, and 1,185. But to pretend to be able to express legitimate concern among 1,184,218, 1,184,219, and 1,184,220 is utter foolishness.

Scientists and engineers are aware of this phenomenon. For this and other reasons, an engineer would express this number in terms of order of magnitude (power of ten): 1.18×10^4 or, if incredible precision were desired, 1.1842×10^4. By looking at the superscript 4, the reader immediately knows that the number is the fourth order of magnitude (ten thousand). By looking at the significant figures, one knows that 1.1 (or 1.18 or 1.184 or 1.1842) tens of thousands are involved.

While scientific notation of numbers helps immensely with significant figures, it does not help most of us with very large or very small numbers. For example, most of us readily understand proportion, and with that understanding we are able to see intuitively the truth of the proposition that 2 is to 4 as 3 is to 6,—that is, each represents the decimal fraction 0.5. But when we see it alleged that 1,000 is to 1,000,000 as 10^{100} is to 10^{103}, most of us doubt until we reason it through. Yet both yield the decimal fraction 0.001 (1×10^{-3})—one one-thousandth.

These human weaknesses are important to understand whenever we discuss the concepts of risk and hazard as well as the concepts of cost and benefit. Failure to apply such understanding can, and does, lead to absurd social consequences.

That is, difficulty in dealing with very small numbers, one in a million (1.0×10^{-6} or 0.000001), for example, sometimes causes us to label as a "hazard" something that in fact is quite remote. Similarly, failure to appreciate the enormity of very large numbers sometimes causes us to fail to appreciate the social cost of a course of action. It may be that $400 billion, for example, doesn't seem overwhelming. As the late Senator Everett Dirksen is said to have quipped, however, "A billion here, a billion there, pretty soon you're talking about real money."

TWO
LEGAL MATTERS

A majority of U.S. schools are faced with some perplexing legal problems that have profound economic implications for schools and for those responsible for running schools. The most immediate and obvious of these problems may seem to some to be the class action to which every U.S. public and private primary and secondary school is a party at this writing, save a few who already have "opted out" or have settled. However, there are more serious and more immediate problems.

For simple examples, what is the legal exposure of a school board that is aware of an asbestos problem but fails to act? Or what may be the future exposure of a board that continues to order and use asbestos products, such as brake linings in a class in auto mechanics? Or what problems arise if a contractor or subcontractor removes asbestos improperly? In each instance, is responsibility limited to students, teachers, and other staff only? How about parents or others merely passing through the school premises? There is legal precedent that poses possible civil and criminal responsibility to the property owner and property manager in every one of these not so hypothetical questions.

More complex examples would include the emerging concern that fibrous glass and other asbestos substitutes may prove more harmful than asbestos and the emerging tendency toward ex post facto legal responsibility.

THE LEGAL FOUNDATION

In this chapter there are presented in brief some fairly sophisticated legal concepts. They are better understood in the perspective of some basic principles of tort and contract law. The importance of understanding these principles also is worthy of note.

Law does not operate in a vacuum. Unless decision makers have an understanding of the basic legal principles, decisions can be made that exacerbate rather than ameliorate a problem.

Recovery against school authorities and the individuals involved is founded in tort law. Theories against suppliers of asbestos have succeeded under both tort and contract law. The principal differences between the two, for practical purposes, are that under tort law punitive damages may be recovered on top of actual damages and that the statute of limitations in contract law begins to run from the day of breach, whereas in tort it begins to run from the day the plaintiff knew or should have known of his or her injury.

Under both contract and tort law, the essence applicable to asbestos litigation is that the defendant breached a duty to the plaintiff. Under modern contract law the contract breach usually is said to arise under the implied warranty of fitness contained in every contract for sale of goods. Plaintiffs still are prevailing under this theory in some states, despite the seemingly impossible hurdle of the statute of limitations.

While there are many tort theories that have succeeded against asbestos companies, the two most common have been the popular tort of "negligence" and the theory of strict liability in case of a failure to warn.

In olden days it was difficult for plaintiffs not in "privity" with defendants to recover. Thus, if A were to manufacture a defective ax through negligence and sell the ax to B, who in turn sold the ax to C, who was injured by the defect, C could not recover against A. Whatever duty may have existed was said to exist only between the parties having contact with each other. The landmark decision abolishing privity and extending the duty to the ultimate purchaser is regarded by many as the case of *MacPherson* v. *Buick Motor Co.*, decided in New York in 1916, in which it was eloquently explained that the world may have become too complicated for us to limit ourselves with principles of privity.

Therefore, asbestos manufacturers (chosen because they had the deepest pockets in sight) have been subject to a duty not to cause foreseeable harm to ultimate purchasers of their products or to those in the vicinity of the product's probable use.

Despite the demise of privity, it still was difficult for C to prove

A's negligence. This problem has been resolved in most instances with a theory of strict liability, particularly as to things that are deemed to be inherently dangerous and that are sold without adequate warning.

The law today regards asbestos, in any quantity, as inherently dangerous. In today's legal environment a manufacturer has a duty to test a product to discover its dangerous propensities, to the standard of an expert in the field, and to warn of the unreasonable dangers that the manufacturer knows or should know will arise from use of the product. That the manufacturers breached this duty in one way or another, or failed to warn adequately, has been established as a matter of law repeatedly in recent years.

In addition to showing a duty, plaintiffs must show injury. In the early asbestos cases, "cause" was extremely difficult to prove. Opposing experts would drone on and the jury would decide whom to believe. The cases are much easier today. Injury from friable asbestos has been pronounced by Congress, several states, and many courts as a matter of law.

THE CLASS ACTION

Prior to August 1, 1987, roughly 30,000 public school districts and private schools will have had to decide whether to participate in a "class action," a case called *In re School Asbestos Litigation*.

Plaintiffs in *In re School Asbestos Litigation* are all public and private primary and secondary schools in the United States. Defendants are essentially every asbestos manufacturing company save the three that already are in bankruptcy. Two defendants already have "settled" for $4.5 million ($4.5x10^6$). It is estimated that they were responsible for less than 0.10 percent of the market ($1.0x10^{-3}$). If the estimates are accurate, the case may be "worth" some $4.5 billion ($4.5x10^9$), probably not enough to handle the total school abatement problem but a lot.

Begun in 1983, *In re School Asbestos Litigation* will require roughly an additional decade for resolution. If plaintiffs are successful, the case will bankrupt virtually every defendant.

Class actions were a judicial creation some 300 years ago. A class action is simply a means of adjudicating common issues for a large number of parties in a single trial. Normally we think of a lawsuit as one plaintiff suing one defendant. Where the number of plaintiffs or defendants becomes too large for the court to handle, the only way for the case to go forward is for the court to deal with representatives of the large number of parties, a procedure known as a class action.

The final judgment in a class action, whether favorable or not, binds all the enumerated members of the class save those class members who have elected not to be represented and bound by the representative's judgment in the suit. Rules relating to class actions in federal courts, such as *In re Asbestos School Litigation*, are embodied in Rule 23 of the Federal Rules of Civil Procedure.

The rules provide that as soon as practicable after the plaintiffs file suit in the form of a class action, the court is required to determine whether to "certify" the suit, that is, whether to allow the action to continue in the form of a class action. Determination that a suit may be maintained as a class action can be changed by the court at a later date, whereupon the class is "decertified." Decertification occurs more frequently than one might imagine, because the very power to change tends to cause many courts to be quite liberal in determining class action status.

Decertification is more than a mere possibility in *In re School Asbestos Litigation*. The Third Circuit Court of Appeals, which already has examined several aspects of the case, has expressed grave doubts as to whether the case is manageable as a class action.

Whatever statutes of limitations are pertinent to an action are "tolled" (that is, they cease to run) while a class action is pending. Thus, if a school had a cause of action in 1983, when *In re School Asbestos Litigation* commenced, the school district does not "opt out," and the class comes to be decertified six years hence, the statute of limitations situation would become as it was nine years before for purposes of that school district being able to bring an independent action.

Classes may be certified in subclasses. In *In re School Asbestos Litigation* this is likely to occur at the time of the initial certification. It is said that there will be several classes of plaintiffs and at least two classes of defendants—those who made "spray-on" asbestos products, and all others. It is quite likely that there will be additional classes and subclasses of plaintiffs as the case progresses.

There are several factors to be considered in determining certification of a class. The factors are pertinent to formation of subclasses as well, one in particular being of importance: that all members of the class must have questions of law and fact in common for resolution by the court.

In *In re School Asbestos Litigation* there are claims sounding in tort law and contract law, both of which are matters of state law and both of which contain idiosyncrasies and outright differences in every state of the union. In addition, state law relating to public procurement frequently is different from the law relating to private procurement. Since both public and private primary and secondary schools are included in *In re School Asbestos Litigation*, additional classes may arise.

States differ in their procurement practices, as do private schools. Some may have required, for example, extensive product warranties while others may not.

In some schools the asbestos present may have been required by state law (for instance, in generically written building codes) at the time of construction, while in others the codes may have been written functionally so as to permit materials other than asbestos that would meet the performance specifications. In some states the foregoing distinction may be irrelevant as a matter of law. In others, however, the distinction may form the basis for a solid defense.

Some school managements may know from whom their asbestos was purchased. Some may not. The difference may become the basis for a subclass or sub-subclass of plaintiffs.

The statute of limitations will vary from state to state. In addition, of course, within each state the application of the statute may be favorable to some schools and not to others. It is possible that this distinction would be the basis for separate subclasses. In most jurisdictions the statute of limitations with regard to torts begins to run when the plaintiff learns of his or her injury or reasonably should have learned through reasonable diligence. Courts have been quite lenient with asbestos plaintiffs on this score.

One classic defense used in some tort cases is known as "assumption of the risk." Most asbestos cases decided to date have involved workers of limited educational background to whom the defense has been held not to be available. For many more sophisticated plaintiffs, however, the defense has been allowed. In those cases the defendant was able to show that the plaintiff had knowledge of the danger of asbestos, appreciated the nature or extent of the danger, and voluntarily exposed himself or herself to the danger. In states in which this defense has vitality, it may well be the basis for formation of a subclass.

As is set forth in Chapter 4, the federal government has a program for grants and loans to assist public and private schools with asbestos abatement. This program was first authorized (but never funded) under the Asbestos School Hazard Detection and Control Act of 1980. Under that act, schools that would have received funds would have been required to assign their claims, if any, against third parties to the federal government. The attorney general was directed to report to Congress within one year on all the possible theories of recovery and chances of success.

The resulting report from the attorney general, dated September 21, 1981, is available through the National Technical Information Service of the Department of Commerce. Though there have been many important developments in the interim, the 232-page report provides an excellent starting point for counsel to a school to begin his analysis.

Two pieces of underscored advice in the attorney general's report are worthy of note here.

First, one of the most promising causes of action described in the report is in "restitution." This action will not lie, however, unless demand has been made for restitution. Therefore, any school authority faced with any degree of expenditure for asbestos abatement should make demand for restitution, prior to self-help, from all concerned with installation of the asbestos. Whether or not a school district is participating in the class action, demand should be made immediately. Making demand costs nothing. FAILURE TO MAKE DEMAND MAY MEAN LOSS OF THE MOST PROMISING SOURCE OF FINANCIAL RELIEF. It should be noted that restitution actions have not fared well so far. Demand is a factor in warranty actions as well, however, and should be made.

Second, also as a matter of the utmost urgency, if time remains to do so, school authorities should consult immediately with qualified counsel to determine whether they should file suit on their own or stay with the class action.

To the casual observer, it may appear obvious that remaining in the *In re School Asbestos Litigation* action is most expeditious. It costs nothing. The apparent stakes are huge. All one has to do is sit back and wait. Most of all, the school authority's political constituency, whether it be the body politic, a governor, a board of trustees, or a bishop, may reason the same way and be furious to learn of a decision not to participate in a "free ride."

On closer examination, however, the decision is far from obvious. In capsule, experienced counsel probably will advise that a very strong case should "opt out" of the class action and proceed independently, while those with very weak cases should stay in and hope to have their weaknesses go unnoticed in the confusion. Only the middle ground case probably will be said to involve an agonizing decision. Tugging in one direction against counsel's advice may be political reality. And in the other direction there may be moral considerations, as noted in Chapter 5 and at the end of this one. Counsel's advice as described, however, does not withstand careful analysis.

The real dilemma lies in budgetary considerations. Asbestos must be abated as a matter of federal law, and of state law as well in some jurisdictions. The budgetary aspect includes the obvious cost of removal and the exposure to fines and penalties if removal does not occur with dispatch. If the money must be spent on abatement, it probably makes economic sense to try to get that money back as soon as possible. For some school authorities, getting outside financial support may be the only way to achieve abatement. The *In re School Asbestos Litigation* class action is not the way to get money fast. Nor, under most reasonable assumptions, is participation in the class action the intelligent decision, regardless of how strong the case may be. Consider the matrix shown in Table 1, prepared by the authors.

Table One
Value of a Hypothetical $1,000 Claim,
Varying Assumptions

	Strong Case		Med. Case		Weak Case	
	Alone	*Class*	*Alone*	*Class*	*Alone*	*Class*
Face value of claim (thousands of dollars)	1.00	1.00	1.00	1.00	1.00	1.00
Probability of favorable judgment	0.90	0.80	0.50	0.50	0.10	0.40

Portion of judgment likely to collect	0.90	0.10	0.90	0.10	0.90	0.10
Estimated costs of collection	0.30	0.30	0.30	0.30	0.30	0.30
Discounted face value of claim	0.57	0.06	0.31	0.04	0.06	0.03
Estimated time from claim to collection (years)	2.00	10.00	2.00	10.00	2.00	10.00
Hypothetical time value of money	0.10	0.10	0.10	0.10	0.10	0.10
Theoretical discounted present value of claim	0.47	0.02	0.26	0.01	0.05	0.01

Face value of claim is the cost of abatement. It is presented as being $1,000 for simplicity.

Probability of favorable judgment is the likelihood of winning. Thus 1.0 would be a certainty of winning, 0.90 would be a 90 percent chance, and so forth.

Portion of judgment likely to collect is the percentage of a winning judgment that is likely to be paid. Very few judgments are paid in full. The losing party, for example, may refrain from appealing in exchange for the winner taking less. Or the losing party may go bankrupt. Or the losing party's assets may be collateral for bank loans, so that nothing is available for satisfying a judgment, thus leading to a compromise amount.

Estimated costs of collection consists of attorney's fees and costs. We have used a 30 percent figure here across the board, applying the 30 percent to the face amount of the claim because applying it to some of the lower numbers yielded a negative net recovery. In fact, cost might be zero because attorney's fees are awarded to the winner in some asbestos cases. As explained elsewhere in this book, the cost of litigating asbestos cases has been very high. Now, however, the cost may be much less as courts begin to take judicial notice of the hazardous nature of asbestos, thus relieving the plaintiff of the burden of such proof.

Discounted face value of claim is a subtotal, taking the face value of the claim and adjusting it for probability of success, a percentage likely to be collected in the event of success, and estimated cost of winning.

Estimated time from claim to collection is an estimate of the time to complete the litigation. This number will vary greatly from state to state in individual cases. However, there is general agreement on the approximate number of years for completion of the class action: ten.

Hypothetical time value of money is an assumed interest rate. This factor is very difficult to predict, but some assumption must be made in order to compare the value of receiving something in the near term with the value of receiving something in the long term. For example, if a school board must borrow in order to abate asbestos, with a view toward repaying all or a portion of the borrowing from a judgment, the time of waiting for reimbursement can be a significant factor.

Theoretical discounted present value of claim is the net result, applying the time value of money to the discounted face value of claim.

Under every situation, going alone has a greater theoretical value than does participating in *In re School Asbestos Litigation.* The very best case shown is only $470 on the $1,000 claim. Further, the differences in theoretical value under the class action are not significant (from $10 to $20) and the theoretical value of recovery in and of itself is not significant.

The probabilities set forth in the table above are very rough approximations. School authorities should use their own estimates of probabilities of winning, value of money, time to collect, and the like, based upon advice of legal and financial counsel. But the analytical approach is correct and the assumptions are not total guesses.

For example, the possibility of collection in the class action is based upon our having taken the total market value of every publicly held defendant (a number far above liquidation value) and having added an estimate of the value of the privately held companies plus an estimate of insurance available to the industry. This total was spread over the total estimated school abatement cost. The resulting number, however rough, probably is overly optimistic. For example, many of the defendants sold products that are not "friable" in the conventional sense. These defendants may be held in a separate class, with little or no responsibility.

Going it alone assumes that no defendant will follow the lead of several other asbestos companies and seek refuge under the bankruptcy laws. In that event, the portion of judgment collectable under going it alone should be reduced to roughly the same as the amount in the class action.

Table 1 makes no allowance for the possibility of punitive damages. Punitive damages have been awarded frequently in asbestos cases. They will not be awarded in the class action, the punitive class already having been excluded on appeal (although those remaining in the class action are free to pursue punitive damages in independent actions). The possibility of punitive damages enhances the "going it alone" column values and should be considered, on advice of counsel, in the analysis. However, recent cases have tended not to award punitive damages.

Different assumptions will yield different results, but any reasonable set of assumptions is likely to yield similar comparative results that will speak for opting out.

If one has property built before 1954 in which the asbestos was supplied by Owens-Illinois (the principal settling defendant, which left the business in 1954), one has an additional problem. Will the $4.5 million pool (which is gathering interest) eventually be earmarked for those who actually used Owens-Illinois product? Or will the pool be spread over all plaintiffs' claims? The "opt out" decision will have to be made before these questions are answered. A similar conundrum exists for purchasers from a smaller settling defendant, Proko Industries, Inc.

An additional complicating factor for everyone is a moral one—not the moral factor described in Chapter 5 but one relating to social efficiency. There is enormous social waste involved in multitudinous actions. The social prospect of trying essentially the same facts and arguing essentially the same law thousands of times before thousands of juries involves monumental waste.

In addition to the waste of financial and human resources, trying individual cases will yield vastly differing results. Some will recover nothing, some will recover windfalls.

The implications of all this are treated in great detail in a 1985 report prepared by the Rand Corporation, entitled *Asbestos in Court.* Among the tragic conclusions in that study, recited on page 1, is: "On average, the total cost to plaintiffs and defendants of litigating a claim was considerably greater than the amount paid in compensation."

Finally, the Rand Corporation (Santa Monica, California) has a very valuable resource called "SAL" (System for Asbestos Litigation). Using SAL, an attorney can evaluate in seconds the probable "value" of an asbestos-based claim. The SAL system merely requires that one input the facts of the particular case. SAL's artificial intelligence system will ask additional questions if need be. When the needed facts have been inserted, the problem is analyzed, based upon case law, claims adjuster experience, and other information, and the dollar value of the case is stated. SAL is so accurate that it was suggested recently in the *American Bar Association Journal* that settling an asbestos case without checking with SAL to make sure the amount is adequate may be tantamount to malpractice.

REMOVAL

For reasons explained in Chapter 4, encapsulation or containment of asbestos does not make sense in the present legal environment. Therefore, only removal is discussed in this book.

In 1980 Congress directed that all schools should survey their premises and assess the magnitude of whatever asbestos problems may exist. The direction came as part of the Asbestos School Hazard Detection and Control Act (ASHDCA) of 1980. This act also authorized a grant program to assist schools in their detection efforts and a loan program to assist schools in "containment or removal of any materials containing asbestos in school buildings in which such materials pose an imminent hazard to the health and safety of children or employees." Schools obtaining loan funds would have been required to assign to the federal government their legal rights to proceed against others. An elaborate program for reporting results of the investigations back to the secretary of education was established.

The grant and loan provisions of ASHDCA, however, were never funded.

Other provisions of the act included requiring the secretary of education to deliver information packages to schools and requiring the attorney general to report back to Congress on the feasibility of the United States suing the asbestos companies and others who may be responsible for asbestos being in the schools. The resulting 230-page report of the attorney general, dated September 21, is available from the National Technical Information Service. It is an invaluable starting point for legal counsel to schools.

Other federal response is set forth in Chapter 1. Of most imminent concern to school authorities is the 1986 congressional mandate that friable asbestos must be abated. This law was described by the *Washington Post* on October 11, 1986, as follows: "One environmental success story is the passage of legislation requiring the Environmental Protection Agency to issue rules within a year mandating that schools identify and remove any asbestos in their building materials, insulation, ceilings and walls." The *Post* news story violates two rules of journalism: it is editorial in that it characterizes the law as a "success story" and it is inaccurate in that the law mandates either removal or control, and applies only to friable asbestos, leaving the definition of "friable" up to the EPA.

A complete explanation of the 1986 congressional mandate is set forth in Appendix A.

An excellent treatment of the 1986 congressional mandate and the conflicting responsibilities under many state laws is available in a 250-page book published by the Bureau of National Affairs, *Asbestos Abatement: Risks and Responsibilities*. It is available for $75 from BNA, 9435 Key West Avenue, Rockville, Maryland 20850.

The proposed EPA regulations in response to the 1986 congressional mandate are set forth in Appendix B. In essence the regulations require removal of spray-on products and encapsulation or removal of all others, of which there is considerable variety.

Asbestos products used in schools include cement products, plaster, fireproof textiles, vinyl floor tiles, thermal and acoustical insulation, and sprayed materials. These products were the norm prior to 1972. The average life of a school building is 50 years. Little construction was done during World War II and asbestos was rationed in any event, so for practical purposes any school built from 1946 to 1972 is quite likely to contain copious amounts of asbestos. One recent official U.S. government estimate is that there are 13,000 such schools; another, that there are 29,000. Whatever the correct number, it is quite large.

The guiding federal light for asbestos abatement until recently was a 1979 EPA tome entitled *Asbestos-Containing Materials in School Buildings: A Guidance Document*. Congress officially has declared that this document provides inadequate guidance. Whatever estimates have previously been made as to the cost of abatement, one can be certain that such estimates are inadequate.

As the following pages reveal, THERE IS GREAT LEGAL EXPOSURE FOR FAILING TO ABATE, for conducting abatement improperly, and for hiring someone to abate who abates improperly. In Chapter 4, there are rules of thumb for estimating the cost of abatement.

Taking all this information together, school authorities can make some sensible decisions as to removal. For example, for a very old school building, removal may make no sense at all. The better course may be to sell the school and let someone else worry about the abatement problem. Indeed, when one places some reasonable value on the risk of engaging in removal and when one realizes that no satisfactory insurance from a rated insurer is available to cushion the exposure, sale will be the appropriate route in most situations. If one were to add in a factor for the possibility of extremely expensive changes in the rules in the near future, sale probably will be particularly attractive.

SCHOOL EXPOSURE

School exposure to legal liability is great, and it comes not just from students and other private citizens who may have breathed a fiber of asbestos on the premises.

The EPA began aggressively pursuing school districts even before abatement became mandatory. For example, in 1984 the EPA obtained a $237,500 fine against the Board of Education of the City of New York, even though New York State's legislative abatement concern preceded that of Congress by one year and the EPA acknowledged that New York City had been "aggressive" in its removal program. For another example, a high school in Duchess County, New York, was closed by court action in April 1984 because it had asbestos ceiling tiles.

Legal exposure exists in the process of removal as well, and insurance should be considered, for there is case law supporting the proposition that the building owner is responsible for the mishaps of the removal contractor, even when the building is being demolished. There also have been several instances of criminal responsibility. Congress greatly ameliorated these risks as part of its 1986 mandate (see Appendix A) by eliminating joint liability and by limiting liability to instances of actual negligence.

Congress made no attempt to limit liability for failure to abate, however, and it is here that the greatest risks lie.

Potential civil liability of schools varies from state to state and is a subject that should be scrutinized carefully by counsel to every school. It is a great mistake merely to rely upon the old common law rule of sovereign immunity (the general rule that government may not be sued without its consent). Private schools, of course, have no immunity defense whatsoever.

In addition, the facts will vary greatly from situation to situation. For example, it has been ascertained by the Justice Department that at least some school boards were not aware that the products applied in their schools contained asbestos. In most, on the other hand, asbestos was specified, either as a legal requirement or by voluntary choice. Such factors may have great bearing upon potential school board liability.

Consider the following hypothetical situation. Jones, head of the state building inspection unit, tells Smith, principal of Public School 113, that the school has been damaged by a recent ground tremor and is certain to collapse the next time it is exposed to a west wind of more than 10 knots. Smith reports the conversation to the school board. Without dissent, it is decided that school must go on and the warning will not be heeded. A few days later the weather bureau forecasts gale force west winds for the following day. During that day the school collapses, causing student Brown to become a paraplegic for life. Does student Brown have a cause of action against the school system? Against the individual members of the school board? Against Smith? Could student Brown reasonably hope for punitive damages as well as actual damages?

The answer to all these questions, in most states, is "yes."

Our general rule that government may be sued only with its own consent flows from the Anglo-American legal fiction that "the king can do no wrong." This rule, which permeates property and contract law, was founded in reasoning that all individual rights flowed from the sovereign's power. Thus the use of that power against the government itself was prohibited and government could be sued only with its own consent.

All government bodies in charge of public schools are within the definition of "sovereign." Several arguments have been advanced in support of the conclusion, including the following. Schools are acting for the benefit of the state and public, and consequently partake of the state's sovereignty with respect to tort liability. There are no means for schools to pay for their torts because the only funds available are those provided for school purposes, and paying for torts is not a school purpose. The school has no right to hurt anyone, so when a school's agent hurts someone, he or she is not acting within the scope of his or her authority and the school cannot be held liable. Public education is for the benefit of all, and welfare of the few must be sacrificed in the public interest.

All these arguments are somewhat circular and have eroded to varying degrees in recent years. In some states the courts have introduced a variety of fictions and artificial distinctions to further circularize the arguments to result in tort liability.

If all this seems confusing, that's because it is. For example, the most common theories used to provide exception to the sovereign immunity rule involve artificial distinctions between governmental and proprietary functions, discretionary and ministerial tasks (the former, believe it or not, retaining immunity), nuisance theory, negligence and willful and intentional misconduct. But the cases are very mixed.

Liability has been found when an eight-year-old fell off a balance beam that was standard gymnastic equipment purchased from a leading manufacturer; when a student injured himself by falling from a nonfunctional fire escape that had not been removed but was off limits to students; when injuries stemmed from failure to maintain an adequate railing on stairs, failure to repair playground fences, and failure to clear an uneven sidewalk of ice; and, on an absolute liability theory (such as that being used against asbestos companies), when an eight-year-old was injured by explosive chemicals stolen from a school by thieves and abandoned on school grounds.

However, liability has not been found (in a nonschool case) when a state-owned chemical plant failed to install legally required health protection for employees and when a music teacher contracted a serious disease after being required, against her will, to use a room and pitchpipe that had been used immediately before by another teacher known by the administration to have a contagious disease.

In addition to civil liability there is potential criminal liability. Building owners have been indicted, for example, for failure to give proper notice of removal activity. It is not a far cry for such owners to be indicted for failure to remove in a timely fashion.

Perhaps the most serious exposure is under CERCLA, described later in this chapter, which may empower the federal government (and certain others) to force their way in, perform the abatement as they see fit, and collect the cost from the owner and the responsible individuals associated with the owner. CERCLA, for practical reasons, may be of most concern to private schools. CERCLA-type liability is partly ameliorated and partly reinforced under the 1986 congressional mandate (see Appendix A).

As noted briefly above, the 1986 mandate also affords potentially great relief for school authorities who strictly follow the procedures called for under the Act. Section 210 of the law, which preempts state law, relieves such authorities from damages for personal injury or property damage resulting from abatement activities, unless negligence is involved, and also precludes joint liability (that is, if the contractor is negligent, the school authority may not be held liable for the contractor's negligence). However, the Act specifically states that this protection does not extend to "acts or omissions not required by the legislation." Reading this language with the Act as a whole, it is clear that the protection does not extend to failure to abate in a timely fashion.

PERSONAL EXPOSURE

Of perhaps greatest concern to school management should be the potential for personal liability.

One state, Tennessee, enacted a law in 1986 creating immunity from liability for acts and omissions by local education agencies' employees arising from detection, management, or removal of asbestos from buildings and requiring the state attorney general to provide defense for such persons. Curiously, the act also commissions a study of the potential for such liability and appropriate methods for protecting such employees. Other states are said to be considering similar legislation.

The reason for the Tennessee action is simple. The general rule is that governmental officers and employees are personally liable for their torts, even where the governmental unit itself may be protected by the immunity doctrine. In most jurisdictions, however, the rule is different for individual members of a school board in relation to acts done as a board or in the discharge of their duties. The exceptions are those relating to the schools themselves, noted in prior pages and, of course, under CERCLA, described elsewhere in this chapter.

This immunity is eroding. For example, in one recent case in which the board of education itself was held to be immune, the principal, the janitor, the maintenance supervisor, and the individual school board members were held responsible for injury to a student occurring when hot water emerged from a drinking fountain improperly installed by an independent contractor. Similar holdings have arisen: when a child was struck by a defective swing; when a student injured himself hammering a nail; when a student pulled a bank of lockers over on himself (agents of the school board only and not the members of the board); and when a student was killed by another student.

In virtually every state, exceptions arise and impose personal responsibility whenever the conduct was willful or wanton or grossly negligent. In our example above of Brown's possible cause of action against Smith and the school board, clearly the board's conduct would cause the individual members to be liable under a willful, wanton, or grossly negligent standard. Is there not an analogy to be drawn between Jones's warning to the school about the danger of collapse and the mandate of Congress, the courts, and several federal agencies to the effect that there is no safe level of asbestos?

The answer most certainly is "yes." There is great potential personal exposure for all in authority unless abatement is undertaken immediately.

In the event that abatement is not undertaken immediately, individuals in positions of authority should at least make their voices known in favor of abatement and would be better advised to resign, unless they are people of modest circumstances for whom personal bankruptcy would be no more than a minor inconvenience.

As noted in Chapter 4, one creative way to obtain financial assistance can involve a "friendly" suit against school authorities who in turn can join those who supplied the asbestos and seek indemnification. Individuals agreeing to such a course should make sure they are covered for their legal expenses and any resulting judgment for the possible event that the prospective indemnifying parties should seek bankruptcy protection. Agreements to provide such coverage probably are illegal, however, under CERCLA (described below), and therefore would be unenforceable if ever contested.

One type of suit that has become very popular is based upon mere exposure to asbestos. This action, believed to have been brought first in Pennsylvania in 1980, seeks a fund to be set aside to compensate for the cancer or other malady that may ensue, plus immediate damages for the mental anguish that will be endured during the 35-year latency period that is said to begin with first exposure.

This type of suit is the single most serious threat to school authorities who fail to abate promptly.

The protection against suit given to school authorities under the Asbestos Hazard Emergency Response Act of 1986 (AHERA) is not afforded to individuals in school management.

CONTRACTOR EXPOSURE

At first blush it may appear to be of no concern to school

authorities what sort of liability an abatement contractor may suffer. However, several cases have held the building owner responsible for the malfeasance of the contractor. Therefore, the contractor's problems become your problems. And the contractors have problems in abundance.

AHERA affords great relief to part of the contractors' problems and to school authorities as well. If the provisions of that act are followed, damages for personal injury or property damage resulting from abatement activity may not be recovered unless negligence is involved. Moreover, joint liability will not be permitted, as explained above in the section "School Exposure." As important as this legislative relief is, other potential problems remain.

Asbestos being a hazardous substance within the CERCLA definition, the school is responsible for the removed asbestos wherever it goes, forever. Thus, if the removal contractor dumps the asbestos-containing spoil in other than a certified disposal site (or in a certified disposal site that later runs afoul of the law and is abandoned), the school can be held responsible for the subsequent cleanup costs.

"Well," you say, "we'll be sure to deal with a big, financially responsible, well-insured abatement contractor." That would be fine, except there aren't any. Large companies that have attempted abatement have been told by their liability carriers that they will either cease such work or have their insurance canceled. All the players, therefore, are both relatively new and relatively small.

Insurance is available, but its limits are so low and the coverage so narrow that it is really not worth having.

In addition, it is virtually impossible for contractors to obtain financing from conventional sources. Contractors are required, therefore, to "bootstrap" their operations. This is what Ms. Harvey's company, Waste Environmental Technology, Inc., did. Only when its sole need for money was for dramatic growth were large amounts of capital available. And, while the company is now more than adequately financed and has been able to attract good officers and directors, obtaining them was most difficult because of the legitimate fear of personal exposure.

The source of all this confusion is an act of Congress designed to "help" people. The act has had the effect of making it extraordinarily difficult for people such as school authorities to handle their abatement problems. How it all happened is worthy of brief description.

The Resource Conservation and Recovery Act of 1976 (popularly known as RCRA) applied prospectively to generators and transporters of hazardous waste and retrospectively to such persons who were guilty of negligence or other legal transgressions. Later Congress passed the Comprehensive Environmental Response, Compensation and Liability Act of 1980 (popularly known as CERCLA) to impose liability without fault, retrospectively and prospectively, under terms of strict liability. Persons liable are all "covered persons," a term that has come to mean, by judicial interpretation, even investors who have a role in management.

Banks and professional venture investors insist upon elaborate contractual provisions that amount to "control" of many aspects of a business. For example, it is normal for such agreements to provide for the lender's or investor's prior approval of salary increases, equipment purchases, contracts over a threshold amount, hiring of persons over a certain salary level, and the like. In addition, it is not unusual for banks and venture investors to insist upon periodic visits and freedom to advise the customer as to his or her operations. It is this sort of comprehensive relationship that courts have used to hold investors liable under CERCLA.

CERCLA covers all hazardous wastes, and asbestos is deemed as a matter of law to be such a waste by virtue of the Clean Air Act, the Clean Water Act, and the Toxic Substances Control Act. There is no specification in CERCLA as to the amount of waste necessary to impose liability on a covered person. One court has stated, however, that while disposal of a penny (copper compounds are hazardous wastes under the Federal Water Pollution Control Act amendments to the Clean Water Act) would probably not warrant liability for cleaning up a site, leaving one pound of pennies on a vacant lot would do so, since one pound is the threshold standard under the Act. After a few days of "acid rain," the leaching from the pennies could require removal of many cubic yards of earth for storage at a hazardous waste disposal site at the cost of many hundreds of thousands of dollars. The court noted the drastic and absurd result but stated that the law is clear.

While CERCLA applies only to the cost of removal and cleanup and not to recovery to third parties damaged in the process, the exposure still is great enough to scare away most sophisticated investors.

THREE
FACTUAL MATTERS

In this chapter there are some facts about asbestos and other natural "hazards," man-made hazards, and probabilities, cost and benefit. This chapter is solely for the reader who may want to know more about asbestos than about the legal environment.

The essence of this chapter is that the perception of hazard from asbestos in buildings is a major popular delusion.

One of Mr. Rollinson's favorite books is *Extraordinary Popular Delusions and the Madness of Crowds*, written by an English lawyer, Charles MacKay, and first published in 1841. The edition in the library at his law firm is labeled "Volume 1"; we do not know whether any other volumes were written. Volume 1 was copyrighted in the United States in 1932 and is now in its twenty-first printing.

A similar work entitled "Extraordinary Popular Delusions, Past and Present" (*Armed Forces Journal International*, January 1978; reprinted in condensation, *Technology Review*, March/April 1978) draws parallels between delusions past and present. The old ones are funny. The new ones are not. (Which undoubtedly is why Mr. MacKay's work has been so popular and the others have not.) Had the asbestos situation in this country today existed at the time of MacKay's writing, surely it would have been included because all of the elements and causes of popular delusions seem to be present in regard to asbestos in buildings.

It is said that there are four reasons there are so many popular delusions (a delusion being a false, persistent belief not supported by sensory evidence): (1) none of us has the time or capability to rethink every single generally accepted proposition; (2) many popular delusions just don't make much difference; (3) the falsity of many delusions involves "unthinkable" thoughts; and (4) many popular delusions appear to be supported by some evidence, usually in the nature of *post hoc, ergo propter hoc* (after the thing, therefore because of the thing) reasoning.

Each of the foregoing is worthy of illustration. The first is unavoidable. For example, while each of us knows in a general way how the gross national product is calculated, none of us has the time to check the numbers. They may or may not give rise to a popular delusion.

The second can be illustrated by the "well-dressed woman." No reasoning person would suggest that someone wearing pointed high heels and mascara is well dressed from any standpoint save the delusions of fashion of the day.

The third, the "unthinkable," has been illustrated frequently by a famous Stanford University logician and teacher, James L. Adams. In his 1974 book *Conceptual Blockbusting* (San Francisco, W. H. Freeman and Company), he describes a barren concrete room full of people. The chamber is lit by a single incandescent bulb screwed into a permanent ceiling receptacle. From the floor protrudes some two feet of a stainless steel pipe, firmly imbedded in the cement. At the bottom of the pipe is a Ping-Pong ball. The inside diameter of the pipe is just sufficient to have permitted the ball to fall free to the bottom. The only implements in the room are a 12-foot length of rope, an ax, an ordinary screwdriver, and a stilson wrench. The people will not be permitted to leave the room until they have extracted the Ping-Pong ball from the pipe. The solution is simple, of course. Each person in the room relieves himself in the pipe until the ball floats to the top and can be flipped away with the screwdriver.

Mr. Adams claims that only one person in his classes has thought of the solution, though a handful have come forward afterward and claimed they were too bashful to speak. The reason the answer is so difficult is that it involves "unthinkable" thoughts.

The delusions that appear to be supported by some evidence are the most pernicious. They always seem to be supported by common sense (the faculty that leads to the delusion that the world is flat).

Our treatment of asbestos seems to stem from a delusion based on a combination of all factors — complication, fashion, unthinkability, and common sense. The "science" that leads to our conclusions is too complicated for most of us to challenge. It is fashionable to condemn asbestos. We appear to have elected to try to live in a risk-free society (a delusion based upon the impossible proposition that reward is possible without risk), and it has become unthinkable to argue that the loss of a single human life is an acceptable factor in any cost-benefit analysis. Since there is evidence that prolonged and intense exposure to asbestos dust can cause lung problems, common sense says that there must be some risk in being exposed to any at all.

That an asbestos particle was found at the heart of each of the tumors that killed heavy smoker Steve McQueen and that he wore an asbestos face mask as a race driver is proof enough that merely a few breathed particles "cause" death. That thousands of other drivers wore similar masks, without observable adverse effects, and that scores have thereby been saved fatal breathing of fire, is irrelevant to most of our thinking.

For more than a score of years this country has been enamored with a proposition that total safety is a near God-given right. Until this delusion passes, those who protest to the contrary expose themselves to possibly extreme ridicule and great financial responsibility. Only the greatest moral strength can stand under such circumstances.

OF ASBESTOS, DUST, AND OTHER NATURAL PHENOMENA

Almost anything taken to excess causes problems of some sort, yet most things in moderation serve a useful purpose. Take dust, for example.

At the nucleus of every raindrop, snowflake, and dewdrop is a particle of dust, a solid less than 2.5 millionths of a meter in diameter, previously suspended in air. Without dust we would have no naturally fresh water.

Natural sources of dust include volcanoes, forest fires, ocean spray, soil and rock (such as asbestos) erosion, and plant spores. Man-made sources include industrial abrasion and grinding operations, mining, grading, and burning.

Great dust concentration, many thousands of times that found in ambient air, can, but does not always, cause lung disease. Common examples are pneumoconiosis (black lung) from coal dust, byssinosis (brown lung) from cotton dust, asbestosis from asbestos dust, berylliosis from beryllium dust, and silicosis from silica dust.

It is generally believed that the concentration of dust in the outdoor air is roughly 100 micrograms (thousandth of a gram) per cubic meter near industrial areas and between 25 and 40 micrograms per cubic meter in the country, depending upon the level of wind erosion, protective vegetation, and the like.

In addition to dust, larger particles are found naturally in the air. Seasonal pollen is an excellent example. Dust is from many different sources and is composed of many different substances. Asbestos is one of the substances.

Asbestos fibers of varying sizes found in the air occur naturally and otherwise. It is difficult to measure the amount of asbestos in the air. There are several different measurement techniques of varying quality, and the results are expressed in several different ways, such as "grams per cubic meter," "fibers per cubic meter," and "fibers per cubic centimeter." Translation of the weight and fiber measures is difficult because most of the fiber measurements cannot detect very small particles and substitute estimates for that which cannot be seen. The range of mass measurements of asbestos in city air has ranged from 1,000 to 100,000 micrograms per cubic meter. The differences may be actual or due to measurement error or both.

There is significant evidence that the level of naturally occurring asbestos dust varies greatly. In some rural areas in the Middle East the levels are nearly hazardous. We are unaware of any credible work on the natural range of asbestos in rural environments in the United States. However, no differences in mortality due to specific cancers have been found in the United States in counties with and without natural deposits of asbestos.

The studies of ambient asbestos in cities have widely varying results. However, it is generally accepted that city air contains between 0.00003 and 0.003 asbestos fibers per cubic centimeter (30 to 3,000 fibers per cubic meter), using mass measurements and converting at 30 micrograms per cubic meter.

In studies of certain villages in Turkey in which there are mortality patterns normally associated with asbestos workers and in which the residents carve their homes out of volcanic rock containing asbestiform fibers, puzzling results have been revealed. Most ambient air samples have revealed less than 0.01 fibers per cubic meter except during cleaning of the caves, at which time the range of samples was from normal (under 0.01) to 1.38 fibers per cubic meter.

Comparing the Turkish phenomena with ambient concentrations in U.S. cities is puzzling and was addressed in some detail in 1984 in the report of the Committee on Nonoccupational Health Risks of Asbestiform Fibers, of the Board on Toxicology and Environmental Health Hazards, of the Commission on Life Sciences, of the National Research Council, of the National Academy of Sciences (isn't government nomenclature wonderful?). In the Committee's report, *Nonoccupational Health Risks of Asbestiform Fibers*, at page 118, it is stated: "It is not clear how to account for the higher mesothelioma and lung cancer rates in these villages if the diagnoses and measured environmental exposures are correct. Possible explanations include enhanced ability of the fibers to cause cancer for reasons not yet known, the presence of other, undetected carcinogenic agents, or increased susceptibility if inhalation of the fibers starts in infancy. . . since children are known to have increased susceptibility to the effects of many environmental agents."

OF MAN-MADE AIR FLOTSAM

As mentioned in preceding paragraphs, men's activity, while dwarfed by that of nature (for instance, one large volcanic eruption or one major forest fire), is such that many "pollutants" enter air and water.

Modern man is not as disruptive as was primitive man, who, contrary to contemporary romantic visions, farmed to depletion and extremes of erosion unknown in the modern world, dammed streams to catch spawning fish (and never removed the dams), and was so filthy that the only way life was bearable was to move on from time to time to spoil another area. (A handful of modern scientists have tried to put to rest Jean-Jacques Rousseau's romanticized concept of the "noble savage," including Dr. Jared M. Diamond of the University of California School of Medicine and archaeologist Julio L. Bentancourt of the University of Arizona.)

Many modern environmentalists, in independent writings and in testimony on behalf of plaintiffs, speak of the "immune dysfunction theory." This line of reasoning (which has been rejected by all responsible authorities of which we are aware, including the American Academy of Allergy and Immunology) holds that life today involves receiving unprecedented insults to one's immune system.

One exposure or one insult too many can alter or diminish the immune system, according to the theory, with fatal results. (The legal argument is that he who administers the back-breaking straw should be held to pay — an argument that has succeeded in many courts.) Whether or not the theory will eventually be proven to have some merit, the suggestion that the insults of modern times are greater than in earlier times seems to us to be patently absurd.

We say "seems to us" because no one was measuring until recently. Therefore, any comparative statement must be based upon speculation. Consider, however, that not long ago there was no such thing as an h.v.a.c. (heating, ventilation, and air conditioning) system to continuously filter the air in the home and (for most of us) the work environment. Not too long ago, when one attended church in winter, one brought a bucket of burning coal to heat the pew — without benefit of a "scrubber" to clean the gaseous effluent billowing from every family's sole source of heat. Only fairly recently did most roads become paved, the rule being that in dry weather the dust was insufferable. In short, common sense says that our modern industrial society is cleaner in almost every way than any environment ever has been.

Yet modern man can, and does, add to the variety of substances that can be found in the environment. The greatest offense of most of these is visual pollution — cans and bottles thrown by the road, garbage floating on lakes and rivers, and the like. But some can be quite damaging to other creatures (such as profligate use of DDT) and even to man himself (such as dumping mercury into the human food chain).

A surgeon friend of Mr. Rollinson's once said that babies and people raised in the most pristine of nonfarming rural environments have lovely, soft, pink lungs. All others' lungs are grimy and somewhat brittle, with pools of sludge in the cracks and crevices, particularly those of heavy smokers, coal miners, and those who work the land in relatively arid conditions.

There is no evidence that under present life expectancies the somewhat dusty environment of a city is any worse than that of the country. Indeed, there is a generally observed correlation between intellectual achievement and city levels of dust in the air, though the "cause" probably is the stimulation of city life due to increased opportunity for intellectual intercourse and not the increased ingestion of airborne particulates.

Some of the man-made additions undoubtedly are not healthy. Since modern technology of filtration enables us to keep heavy doses of particulates out of the air on a reasonably economic basis, it probably makes sense to do so, without waiting to find out if heavy and prolonged exposure will cause cancer or some other less serious malady. Mere increased visibility, decreased laundry bills, and greater pleasure from the act of breathing should be sufficient justification.

Some particulate exposure is necessary to life itself — making rain, for example. And the exercise of the bodily functions that dispose of unwanted breathed substances probably is beneficial. Almost anything in excess probably is not beneficial. So it probably makes sense to avoid excess — of purity or of contamination — regardless of the substance involved.

An early observer of the benefits of moderation was one of the great Western iconoclasts, Theophrastus Philippus Aureolus Bombastus von Hohenheim, an early-sixteenth-century physician who called himself Paracelsus. He appears to have been one of the first to promote the concept that disease is caused by external agents that attack the body — a direct confrontation to the then traditional idea of disease as an internal upset of the balance of the body's "humors." His notions were so bizarre in his time that he never obtained a secure academic position or permanent employment. His efforts to make medicines were labeled as "alchemy" at a time when alchemy had fallen into disrepute, even though the work of the alchemists, of course, became the basis for modern chemistry.

Paracelsus wrote that all things are poisons. It was his view that everything has poisonous qualities and only the dose makes a thing a poison. His then heretical views in a general way have proven to be true, a concept that many of us still have difficulty accepting.

An excellent example of Paracelsus's wisdom is found in nicotine. At one extreme in concentration, nicotine is an extremely poisonous, colorless, oily liquid alkaloid used, among other places, in pesticides that, in sufficient dose, can cause respiratory failure and general paralysis in humans. At another extreme, nicotinic acid is a member of the vitamin B group and an important human food supplement. In between, it is either a relaxing and pleasurable delight or a curse on the human race, depending upon whether one has elected to be a user of tobacco.

PROBABILITIES AND PHYSICAL RISKS

Cynics have said that life is a terminal disease, a harsh but true reality.

In Marjorie Kinnan Rawlings' tender Pulitzer Prize-winning novel, *The Yearling*, (Charles Scribner's & Son, New York, 1939) there is an incident at page 235 that brings this home. Jody, the young boy, his father, Penny Baxter, and their neighbors have killed a wildcat and her cubs.

Jody took the limp bodies [of the cubs] and cradled them. "I hate things dying," he said. The men were silent. Penny said slowly, "Nothin's spared son, if that be any comfort to you!"

"Taint."

"Well, it's a stone wall nobody's yet klumb over. You can kick it, and crack your head against it and holler; but nobody'l listen and nobody'l answer."

We tend to speak of "risk" as though it either exists or it does not. Many of us consider that "risk" is to be avoided at all cost, particularly if human life is involved, and many of our laws and regulations of recent years reflect such a belief.

Such a view of the world is sad. Those who elect to live their lives in accord with such a belief (and there are many such people) will never use a surfboard; never take an ocean swim; never ski a mountain trail; never smoke a cigarette; avoid using an automobile except for absolute necessity; never try a new food — in short, they will live depressingly drab lives.

Everyone should be free to live such a life if he or she so desires. However, presumably because misery tends to love company, most people who elect to live such lives tend to try to force such a degree of caution on all around them.

Most people, of course, take many life-threatening risks every day. As to some, there is no choice. As to most, there are many choices. The magnitude of the risk compared with the perceived benefit of taking the risk and the perceived cost of not taking the risk are what is important to most people.

The risk of death from lightning is 35 in 1 million, from tornadoes 49 in 1 million, and from hurricanes 28 in 1 million. Yet millions of perfectly rational people voluntarily live in areas in which these natural phenomena occur. The risk in driving to school is many times greater than the theoretical risk of contracting cancer while in an asbestos-filled building, yet many concerned people not only drive to school but take pleasure drives with children in tow.

In February 1987 the Bureau of National Affairs published in its *Toxics Law Reporter* a beautiful little essay by Paolo F. Ricci and Louis Anthony Cox, Jr., entitled "Acceptability of Chronic Health Risks." The authors make a persuasive case that there are five principal factors in risk acceptability: (1) voluntariness, (2) equity, (3) legal environment, (4) uncertainty, and (5) perceptions. The analysis of each of these factors brings us closer to understanding the seeming irrationality of public reaction to risk.

We think, however, that there is an overriding factor that escaped Ricci and Cox, namely, personal inconvenience. Closely related to the first factor, voluntariness, the concept of personal inconvenience is perhaps the most understandable and the most forgivable. In any society, such as ours, in which individual liberties are highly valued, the notion of having risk imposed upon us tends to be abhorred while the imposition of risk-reducing measures (such as forced wearing of seat belts) tends to be equally disdained. Thus, while Ricci and Cox write of voluntariness in terms of one voluntarily being exposed (or not exposed) to a risk, it is arguable that voluntariness is better understood in the reaction than in the imposition.

It would be hard to understate the extremes of feeling in this regard. Comparison of the following three fact situations may illustrate how drastic our feelings tend to be. Let us consider (1) being a victim of violent crime, (2) contracting cancer from sunlight, and (3) exposure to radon gas emanating from a nuclear processing plant.

According to a study published by the Justice Department in March 1987, a 12-year-old today faces an alarming future. He or she has an 83 percent chance of being a victim of violent crime at least once in his or her lifetime, for example. One out of every 12 of the women in this class will be the victim of a rape or attempted rape. Over 99 percent will be the victim of a personal theft, and 87 percent will be personal theft victims three or more times. Over 75 percent of their households will be burglarized at least once each 20 years of their lives. Twenty percent of them will have their automobile stolen. One in 133 will be a murder victim!

Despite these grim statistics, few of us take the simple precautions that would reduce our exposure, such as barring our windows, never traveling alone or at night, and exercising similar precautions that are well known but expensive and highly inconvenient. We are in control, and most of us opt for taking the risks, as alarming as they are.

The best available estimates of the risk of cancer death from being exposed to natural background radiation is 50 in one million. Increasing our exposure to sunlight drastically increases the risk. Despite this commonly known phenomenon, most of us play out of doors and even sunbathe on occasion.

It is agreed by most that the risk of cancer death from exposure to radon from uncontrolled uranium mill tailings is one in 50 million for the population at large and one in 2,600 for workers exposed on a regular basis. This level of risk has been found to be legally unacceptable when challenged, not by the workers themselves but by "public interest" advocates speaking for the population at large.

All this leads to an interesting analysis, set forth in Table 2, prepared by the authors.

Table Two
Source of Risk of Death

	Murder	Exposure to Natural Radiation	Uranium Tailing Exposure
Probability of event	7.5×10^{-3}	5.0×10^{-5}	2.0×10^{-8}
Social cost of regulation to reduce risk	high	high	very high
Social benefit of regulation to reduce risk	very high	very low	none
Personal cost of regulation to reduce risk	high	high	none
Personal inconvenience of regulation to reduce risk	very high	very high	none

Legal regulation imposed upon activity	none	none	Abolition of activity or extreme control

From this analysis we see that even in the face of incredibly dangerous hazard, most of us take few precautionary measures and impose none on others in instances in which personal inconvenience or cost is involved. Where the burden of cost and inconvenience is perceived as being on others, however, we react harshly to risks that are so remote as to be incomprehensible to most of us, without regard to cost or benefit.

ASBESTOS RISKS

Examining both the theoretical and the actual risks from asbestos in buildings yields very depressing results, particularly in face of the estimated $400 billion that will be required for abatement. The interest alone on this amount would employ some 2 million policemen, more than a fivefold increase in the number of police and detectives in the United States.

To understand the theoretical risk from asbestos, one must understand how that theoretical risk is calculated. First is the assumption that there is no safe threshold level below which there is zero risk from asbestos. Indeed, as you may be shocked to learn, THIS IS THE ASSUMPTION USED BY THE ENVIRONMENTAL PROTECTION AGENCY FOR ALL SUBSTANCES THAT APPEAR TO BE CARCINOGENS WHEN ADMINISTERED IN MONSTROUS OVERDOSE TO MICE (usually the B6C3F1 strain of mice, which have been bred specifically to be susceptible to contracting cancer).

From this untenable assumption, scientists then calculate that the risk is proportional to the exposure and thereby extrapolate a quantitative risk assessment based upon the mortality data from the higher levels. For many purposes, if the estimated hypothetical increase in mortality thus derived is 1 in 1 million or greater, the risk is said to be unacceptable. No cost or benefit typically is considered. If there is a national mania in progress, as with asbestos, no hypothetical increase in mortality is acceptable. Thus, for example, the National Institute of Occupational Safety and Health, competing for the appearance of being concerned for the public safety, has proclaimed that there is no safe level of asbestos exposure.

From these groundless extrapolations we learn that asbestos in schools can be expected to result in deaths from cancer of 10 in 1 million, according to the EPA, and between 1 to 6 in 1 million, according to others.

Since death is a certainty, the meaning of these numbers is best appreciated in terms of reduction of life expectancy. As has been widely published, for example, a heavy smoker is said to have some four years shorter life expectancy than he or she otherwise would have. The above hypothetical numbers for asbestos in schools reveal that, if they were real, students should expect something between a few seconds and three hours shorter life, depending upon whose estimates one uses.

Another way of attempting to put a 1 in 1 million increased risk into perspective is as follows. Since each of us presently has 1 chance in three of contracting cancer in his or her lifetime, an added risk of 1 in 1 million would change a 0.333333 probability to 0.333334.

It is said to be a U.S. weakness to engage in excess. Many people assume, for example, that if two pills will bring calm relief, then four pills should bring a sense of well-being and eight should induce euphoria, when in fact four pills of the otherwise beneficial substance may induce dizziness and eight, brain damage. The theoretical approach described above is an example of the obverse of the same coin. That is, the reasoning is that if decades of breathing too much asbestos dust is harmful, then a moment of such breathing must also be harmful, though possibly less so.

As noted earlier in this book, common sense is indeed the faculty that teaches that the world is flat. However, the world does appear to be flat in the immediate vicinity and the perception of its being so serves reasonably well for most purposes.

Back in the old days, when government allowed us to burn leaves in the fall, it did not take a lot of common sense to learn not to stand downwind from the fire in order to avoid breathing excessive dust. People caught in dust storms usually instinctively figure out that breathing the dust is likely to cause lung problems, and so they cover their faces to breathe. Those exposed to excessive dust in the workplace, whether it be the coal mine, the cotton mill, or the asbestos shop, probably have been, and are, smart enough to figure out that continual breathing of such air would be harmful. They also undoubtedly thought about feeding their families and made a reasoned choice.

Employers in such workplaces essentially have always resisted efforts to force them to keep the air reasonably clean. On an individual basis this is perhaps understandable, for no individual wants to have the highest costs of anyone in the industry. On a group basis there is something sinister about the whole thing, as juries recently have tried to make clear to asbestos companies.

If the tangible evidence against the asbestos industry is accurate, perhaps there is justification for the juries' wrath. However, the industry's conduct should be viewed in the context of societal norms of the day. For example, one of the industry leaders, which allegedly had sponsored extensive research into detection and prevention of lung disease among workers, allegedly wrote in a confidential report in 1949:

It must be remembered that although these men have the X-ray evidence of asbestosis, they are working today and definitely are not disabled from asbestos. They have not been told of this diagnosis for it is felt that as long as the man feels well, is happy at home and at work, and his physical condition remains good, nothing should be said... [A]s long as the man is not disabled,...he can live and work in peace and the Company can benefit by his many years of experience. Should the man be told his condition today there is a very definite possibility that he would become mentally and physically ill, simply through the knowledge that he has asbestosis.

While such a paternalistic attitude today arouses the ire of most who read it, it was not an unusual or condemned attitude in 1949.

But the common sense of one day is the absurdity of the next. The legal situation is not good for those who have been judged to have withheld such information from workers.

The school situation is quite different. The standard of responsibility that has been set and legally recognized has no factual justification whatsoever. The hypothetically derived standard used by the EPA for all substances believed to increase the likelihood of cancer administered in gargantuan doses to cancer-prone mice is not well founded even in theory. And, in fact, there is no evidence whatsoever of harm resulting from the levels of ambient asbestos found in schools.

The National Academy of Sciences, perhaps this nation's most prestigious source of unbiased and scholarly information, in its 1984 report *Nonoccupational Health Risks of Asbestiform Fibers,* said:

For the quantitative risk assessment, a linear model for low dose extrapolation was used. When quantifying risk from nonoccupational exposures,
uncertainties are introduced not only by the selection of mathematical
models but also because the characteristics of fibrous materials in the ambient environment differ from those in the workplace. By converting mass
concentrations measured in the environment to equivalent numbers of
fibers in the workplace, the committee assumed a median population exposure of 0.0004 fibers/cm^3 air throughout a 73-year lifetime. Based on
this and various other assumptions, the individual lifetime risk for lung
cancer was estimated to be less than one in a million, and for mesothelioma
it was approximately nine in a million. However, other assumptions could
decrease the risks essentially to zero, or could increase them.

In other words, no actual evidence of risk is available. All we have
is extrapolation from workplace data, which indeed do show that
over a long period of time exposure to very high levels of asbestos
dust causes problems in some (but not all) people.

The situation was more clearly described in a 1986 article by Frank
B. Cross in the *Columbia Journal of Environmental Law.* The following excerpt, from which massive footnotes are omitted, is a fair statement of the situation.

It is worth repeating at this point that there is no demonstrable evidence
of any harm from asbestos in buildings. One type of disease that might
be traced to school exposures is mesothelioma, because it is caused almost
exclusively by asbestos. Yet Dr. E. Donald Acheson of the University of
Southhampton, the Chairman of the medical subcommittee for the United
Kingdom Advisory Committee on Asbestos, observed that there "is no
evidence up to the present time of cases of mesothelioma having occurred
as a result of exposure in schools." Dr. Henry Anderson, formerly of the
Mt. Sinai Medical Center, likewise stressed that he was "not aware that
there are any mesotheliomas that have been attributed to. . .school asbestos
exposure." Dr. Hans Weill of Tulane University described the risk as "very,
very low if not nonexistent." Dr. Thomas Kurt, an Associate Professor
of Internal Medicine at the University of Texas Health Science Center, stated
that the "issue of exposure to school children is greatly out of proportion
to the actual danger and there is no serious or substantial risk to
schoolchildren." Evidence such as this led the Ontario Royal Commission
to conclude: "We deem the risk which asbestos poses to building occupants
to be insignificant and therefore find that asbestos in building air will almost

never pose a health hazard to building occupants." The New Jersey Asbestos Policy Committee concluded that it "is *very* unlikely that non-occupational exposures...produce mesothelioma" [emphasis in original]. Indeed, numerous governmental and scientific groups, including the National Academy of Sciences, Commission of European Communities, and the International Agency for Research on Cancer, have concluded that low level exposures do not pose significant public health risks.

Some have worried, however, that children may be more susceptible to asbestos-induced disease and that the hypothetical risk assessments may understate actual risk. Theories include observation that children have higher rates of metabolism than adults, that some children tend to be mouth breathers, that children have a higher rate of air exchange, and that children experience rapid multiplication of cells. In fact, there are no data on the subject save evidence from some animal experiments that suggest a contrary conclusion.

One of the best, albeit unwitting, experiments has occurred in Ambler, Pennsylvania, just a few miles outside of Philadelphia. Asbestos has been produced in Ambler for more than 100 years. Next to one of the old plants is a refuse heap containing more than 150,000 tons (1.5×10^8 pounds) of asbestos that has been exposed to the wind and open air for most of its existence. Adjoining the dump has been a school playground; as a result, many thousands of children have played in essentially pure asbestos and breathed heavy doses over the years, varying with weather conditions. Dr. David Roberts, inventor of the Vitrifix process for destroying asbestos fibers, has studied the Ambler situation. He states that there is not a single recorded instance of mesothelioma among Ambler children.

As explained in some detail in Chapter 2, the law is not in accord with physical reality. Congress, for example, stated in 1986, without reservation, that "medical science has not established any minimum level of exposure to asbestos fibers which is considered to be safe to individuals exposed to fibers" and "the presence in school buildings of friable or easily damaged asbestos creates an unwarranted hazard to the health of the school children and school employees who are exposed to such materials."

Similarly, the courts have concluded that as a matter of law, exposure to a single fiber may pose problems of liability. In the Court's words in one of the Johns-Manville cases, for example, it was stated that mesothelioma "may result from one exposure to asbestos dust or fibers" as a matter of law.

FOUR
FINANCIAL
MATTERS

It is quite easy for a layman to make a rough estimate of the cost of asbestos removal. In addition, there are several possible sources of financial help to assist or cover the cost. This chapter addresses both subjects.

Frequently "encapsulation" is considered an economical alternative to actual removal of asbestos. This is a short-term solution and a shortsighted one as well, in our view. However, our views probably are moot. In 1986 Congress directed the EPA to issue rules within one year mandating that all schools identify and encapsulate or remove any possibly hazardous asbestos in their building materials, insulation, ceilings, and walls. (See Appendixes A and B.)

Under present law, therefore, removal will be required eventually, even if one elects to have the building demolished. Encapsulation usually makes the expense of eventual removal greater. Thus, encapsulation is not a sound approach in pure economic terms and the subject is not analyzed in this book.

There are additional reasons why encapsulation would be foolhardy. All substances (even durable asbestos) deteriorate with time. Therefore, encapsulation merely postpones the day when the alleged hazard will exist again. Barring a more moderate legal environment, which does not appear to be in the offing, the most cost-effective approach would be to remove now.

An excellent analysis of the economics of the situation can be found in Donald N. Dewees's book *Controlling Asbestos in Buildings — An Economic Investigation,* published by Resources for the Future in Washington, D.C., and distributed by Johns Hopkins University Press in Baltimore. Reporting on a study by the prestigious Resources for the Future, Dewees states that the risks to health, if any, from asbestos in buildings are so trivial and minor that the expense of removal cannot be justified, but the legal risks are so great as to make immediate abatement mandatory. Were it not for the legal risks, he states, the most cost-effective time to deal with abatement would be at the time of demolition of the building.

Those who get involved with abatement may wonder why none of the larger construction companies ever bid on asbestos removal work. In part the reason is that each job usually is too small to draw attention from major companies. A more important reason, however, is legal in nature. The asbestos abatement contractor is exposed to great risk. Employees sue (no matter how carefully supervised) for ensuing lung problems (regardless of how caused). Passersby who unwittingly walk in on the process can (and frequently do) sue for all sorts of things, including mental anguish for the ensuing 35 years they will wait to contract cancer — to paraphrase from a recent action brought by several doctors and nurses against a Texas hospital and its abatement contractor.

Because of the great legal exposure, abatement must be a single-purpose business. Otherwise, one would put at risk all of the assets employed in other, less risky parts of the business enterprise.

Because asbestos abatement is a relatively new activity and because it must be performed by a single-purpose company, essentially every company in the business is relatively small and new. Because of the newness, each has had to go through a period of being unable to get insurance of any kind until it had experience, and experience can be gained on very few jobs because most customers want an insured contractor.

COST OF REMOVAL

There are many construction situations in which asbestos commonly is found in schools. The cost of removal varies greatly according to the situation, as a function of the difficulty of removal and the cost of replacement. For example, in the spray-on ceiling situation described in this chapter, the range of costs of removal presently is between $5.75 and $30.00 per square foot.

An additional variable results from geographic location. Labor cost is one obvious element, but transportation regulations, distance to the nearest disposal site, and similar factors vary greatly from jurisdiction to jurisdiction.

Another major variable has to do with the cost of insurance and bonding. The experience of the contractor is a factor here, as is the economic size (net worth) of the contractor (most of whom are quite small, for reasons explained above).

Perhaps an even greater factor regarding insurance is the tort law of the state in which the job is to be performed. States with "pot of gold" or "strike it rich" tort law, such as New Jersey, California, and Illinois, will require a much higher premium than will states that adhere to more traditional standards of fault and predictability, such as Virginia and North Carolina.

Speed of required contractor performance also is a major factor. If the job must be done quickly, so as to permit use of the facility again, work around the clock is quite expensive.

The second greatest variable probably is the time of performance. On weekends (because of abatement in otherwise occupied office buildings) and summers (because of abatement in otherwise occupied schools) there is great demand for abatement. Contractors know this and bid much higher for these periods than they do for "off-peak" work.

The greatest variable has to do with the extent to which abatement is conducted. For example, in a recent procurement by the EPA for abatement of ceiling material in a reception area of one of its own buildings, the specifications call for removal of the material and replacement of the carpet in the reception area, and replacement of the heating, ventilating, and air conditioning system in the entire building. With equal logic, one could have called for replacement of carpet throughout the building or, presumably, replacement of the entire structure. The line is almost equally absurd regardless of where it is drawn.

Based upon interviews with engineers who have professional experience in asbestos abatement, our best estimate of the range of costs for the work in the seven most common school situations is approximately as follows:

1. Spray-on ceilings: $5.25 to $30.00 per square foot

2. Pipe insulation: $5.50 to $26.00 per linear foot (partly dependent upon diameter of pipe)

3. Vinyl asbestos tile: about $5.00 per square foot

4. Walls (usually in band rooms, choral rooms, cafeterias): $3.50

to $15 per square foot

5. Lay-in ceiling tiles: $3.50 to $12.00 per square foot

6. Pan and joist coating: $12.00 to $35.00 per square foot

7. Robertson decking: $9.00 to $16.00 per square foot.

An approximate understanding of the components of cost can be gleaned from a breakdown of the most economical removal of spray-on ceilings. We estimate further that the $5.25 per square foot number set forth above consists approximately of the following elements:

Site preparation	$ 0.50
Removal and cleanup	1.00
Bagging, transportation, and disposal	0.75
Replacement	1.25
Certified industrial hygienist	0.25
Insurance	0.50
Bonding	0.25
Overhead and profit	0.75
Total	$ 5.25 per square foot

Some of the reasons the costs are so high may be of interest. Workers must wear disposable clothing and portable respirators. They must work in a totally enclosed environment that includes a facility for removing clothing and showering. At all times the air in the area must be continually evacuated and filtered. For contractor protection (and as a requirement of obtaining insurance) the entire process must be monitored by a certified industrial hygienist (preferably independent) who continually takes and tests air samples to make certain nothing is escaping. The material removed must be bagged and transported under safety conditions approximating the transportation of nuclear materials in early days.

To the foregoing costs, must be added additional indirect costs, such as procuring, printing, and advertising bid specifications; contract monitoring; police overtime to secure the building; moving furniture, books, and the like; and cleaning drapes and furniture. If the EPA regulations are promulgated to the standard that the agency has imposed upon itself in recent procurements, one must add major expenditures for replacing carpet, replacing heating and air-conditioning systems, and similar absurdities.

All of this is to protect against anyone accidentally breathing a single thread of a material that essentially all of us have been breathing in varying quantities all our lives without perceptible mishap.

SOURCES OF HELP

Superficially the easiest source of help is to be found in the *In Re Asbestos School Litigation* class action. As explained earlier in this book, however, that is far from a sure thing and, even if it were, the dollars are likely to be long in coming — more than a decade, in all probability. They won't help with today's budget problems.

Even an independent action, though much faster than the class action, would require significant time. There are sound legal reasons mandating abatement without waiting for third-party help.

There are many other sources of help. The obvious one is to seek assistance under the federal Asbestos School Hazard Abatement Act. Unfortunately, the funds available are limited. The report on 1986 activity was not available at this writing, but the 1985 results are said to be typical. In utilizing the full $50 million in 1985, the EPA: (a) received 8,548 project applications from 1,108 school authorities for 5,095 schools and (b) offered loans or grants to 198 authorities for 417 projects in 340 schools. Agency materials regarding this program state that "Congress intended that Federal Funds go only to school districts with *serious* asbestos hazards and *severe* financial need" (emphasis in original). A large percentage of the funds disbursed has gone to parochial schools.

On March 15, 1987, the president signed a joint congressional resolution requiring the EPA to disburse $47,500,000 for asbestos cleanup during the summer of 1987. On March 18 the EPA sent out 35,000 letters to school districts in response to the presidential order. In a public announcement, however, the Agency made clear that only the districts with the very greatest financial need would be eligible for the funds.

Fortunately, there are many creative solutions.

The most ambitious sort of solution could prove to be a source of long-term revenue for a school district, namely, for the school district, if permitted by law, to facilitate establishment of a facility for destruction of asbestos by reducing it to harmless glass in an electric furnace.

There are two commercially available furnaces for this purpose, both of which are merely glass furnaces modified in several ways, including adding a "scrubber" for cleaning the gaseous effluent coming from foreign material in the asbestos spoil. One is available from Penberthy Electromelt International in Seattle, Washington. The other is from Vitrifix of North America in Washington, D.C. The essence of both processes is that they take asbestos spoil and literally destroy every asbestos fiber and turn it into glass. There are absolutely no harmful by-products of the process.

Unfortunately, EPA regulations presently require that the glass obtained from the melting process be disposed of in a landfill just as if it were asbestos. It is hoped that the regulations will be changed during 1989. Once change is accomplished, processes will eliminate asbestos at a cost competitive with landfill storage. They have the additional advantage of removing forever the fear that someone will come back to the school someday, under CERCLA, because of leakage in the landfill.

If a city school system, say, were to provide a site for a privately owned Vitrifix plant in exchange for the private entity abating asbestos in the schools, the private entity could then serve as a disposal facility for abatement from other government and private buildings. Future rental for such a site might also be possible, thus providing a source of income for the school system.

Other approaches can involve transferring the problem to someone else. For example, most schools containing structural asbestos are quite old. Many of them are located on rather large pieces of property. In recent years many older schools have been developed into residential or commercial condominiums or rental units. Therefore, one solution may be to sell the building to a developer in exchange for his building a new school on another part of the same property. Let him then abate the asbestos as part of his renovation. Under CERCLA there would be an overhanging legal problem, in that improper abatement could come back to haunt the school. But the trade-off may be worthwhile if the buyer is a company of integrity.

Another solution, albeit a political one, may be to go to the state or municipal agency that set the building standards requiring or permitting asbestos, and suggest that the abatement properly should come out of its budget. After all, these are the "experts" who allowed or, in many instances, insisted that asbestos be used. The present administrators or their predecessors were relying, justifiably, upon the expertise. If fault lies anywhere, that is the place.

The ultimate political solution is to go to the state legislature with the foregoing argument. It certainly has appeal.

In some states it may be possible greatly to reduce the cost of abatement by doing the job oneself, under the supervision of a trained expert. The rules to be promulgated by the EPA in 1987 (under congressional mandate in late 1986) may not permit self-help. If self-help is appealing, one might either handle the abatement before the rules are published or lobby for self-help provisions in the rules.

Self-help could be done in a number of ways. For instance, retain a first-class consultant to supervise the work. Seek volunteers from convicts serving time for nonviolent crimes. Let them do the work in exchange for reduced sentences. Do the work without insurance. Mix the spoil on site with cement and with the mixture form large riprap for use in highway roadbeds or in shoreline erosion prevention. In addition to or instead of convict labor, train unemployed volunteers for the task. They will emerge with a skill that is much in demand in private industry.

The University of Alabama has taken the self-help approach, using 45 school employees under supervision of trained experts. Begun in 1985, the Alabama project will take many years, over 200 campus buildings being involved. The Alabama approach will save the school a great deal of money, and the saving may be worth the great legal exposure in the interim.

A particularly creative solution may lie in the law of indemnity—which, incidentally, tends to remove difficult statute of limitations problems. Hornbook and case law on the subject is roughly as follows. When the supplier or manufacturer of an article is actively or primarily negligent by supplying a product that is unreasonably dangerous for the use for which it was made or supplied (which most states now will take asbestos to be as a matter of law), and the person to whom the item is supplied justifiably relied upon the supplier's care but is nevertheless passively or secondarily negligent in causing injury to a third person because of his failure to discover, correct, or remedy the danger (as noted in Chapter 2, a very real threat to school authorities today), the two negligent parties, though both may be liable to the third person, are not in pari delicto, and the one that was passively negligent may maintain an action for indemnity against the one that was actively negligent.

In order to utilize this solution, one would have to arrange for a "friendly" nuisance action seeking to compel abatement to be brought against school authorities. The authorities in turn would join the asbestos supplier. The ultimate financial responsibility would be laid to the supplier, under present law.

A major risk in friendly actions is that they may become not so friendly. Of particular concern in an asbestos situation would be that the friendly plaintiffs might decide to seek more than mere abatement, and go after mental anguish and a fund to provide for them 35 years hence in the event that they contract an asbestos-related disease. Such a change of events would certainly bankrupt the source of indemnity, and in any event the funds would not go where the school authority needs them, namely, to satisfy the legal requirement to abate.

Another solution may be to demand that those supplying the asbestos handle the abatement. While they almost certainly will refuse because of the precedent it would set, one might be able to make a deal along one of the following lines. (Incidentally, private schools are able to make deals in secret, with formidable damages for breach of the secret, thus avoiding the unfavorable precedent problem.)

Traditionally the costs of prosecuting and defending an asbestos case have exceeded the amount awarded. Appeal to the supplier that he will save legal fees and gain lots of good publicity by voluntarily at least assisting in the burden of abatement.

A reasonable "settlement" figure could be on the order of $0.25 on the dollar. While estimates of the amounts netted differ greatly, the best data seem to us to suggest that after counsel fees, expert witness fees, and the like, this is roughly what plaintiffs are recovering, when they recover.

To the extent that school boards and individuals have exposure, as summarized in Chapter 2, so may the supplier of asbestos, perhaps even in the face of otherwise difficult statute of limitations problems. Making demand along these lines could result in a favorable settlement.

In many states there are consumer statutes that award treble damages and legal fees in successful cases involving misleading statements or failures to disclose. While these statutes were enacted to attack "bait and switch" advertising and similar practices, recent cases have held that business transactions are within the purview of the statutes. The threat of such an action might be a useful negotiating tool.

Financial aid is not the only source-of-help problem that schools face. Another problem is to find someone to do the work. There is only a handful of certified and qualified abatement contractors in the country, and the number is not likely to increase dramatically. The problem is so severe that many states, Louisiana, for example, have postponed abatement indefinitely in order to allow time for more contractors to emerge. Government entities are at a particular disadvantage because many are required to procure only on competitive bidding. The better contractors are performing for private industry, schools, and hospitals on a cost-plus basis.

There is a rapidly expanding pool of individuals who are qualified to undertake abatement projects. However, for reasons explained in Chapter 2, financing is not readily available.

Some schools can solve both of these problems with some creative structuring. First, let the work in very small quantities to avoid competitive bidding. This has the additional advantage in some instances of not requiring the expensive around-the-clock work sometimes associated with larger jobs. Second, offer advance funds and progress payments. By and large there are no other sources of financing available to contractors.

If necessary, close the school until abatement can be accomplished. The legal risks of not doing so are too great to suffer.

Typical elementary school with asbestos insulation.

One area of asbestos contamination is the pipe basement or mechanical room.

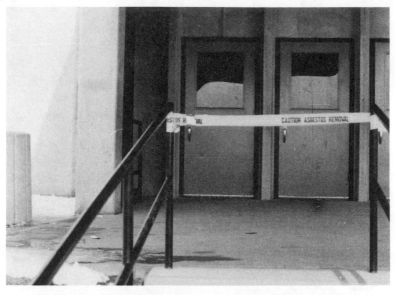

First order of business is to restrict unauthorized personnel from building.

Sprayed on application of asbestos fireproofing in school hallway.

Areas where asbestos materials have delaminated from surfaces.

Frames up with plastic being applied to inside of walls.

Complete inside plastic coverings of hallway.

Inside of wooden frame structure with plastic now covering entire hallway.

All furniture and fixtures must be removed
before plastic can be applied.

Typical room after enclosing in plastic. Asbestos
materials above drop ceiling.

Negative air machine set-up to exchange air in room 3-5 time per hour.

Miniature pumps in 2 locations outside the school building.

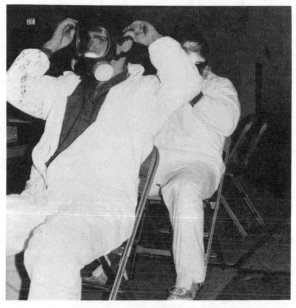

Respirator fit instructions for workers before job.

Structural checking with sprayed on asbestos above drop ceiling. Material is being removed with scrapper.

Worker vacuuming up material as it is scrapped.

Because the material is removed wet, large quantities of water is sprayed in enclosure and must be swabbed from floor.

Final cleaning where worker uses small metal bristle toothbrush to remove material in cracks and hard to get areas.

Swabbing amended water to reduce damage to floors.

Totally cleaned area which has also been sprayed with encapsulant to ensure no fibers can be released.

Supervisor looking in dark corners for residual material during final walkthrough.

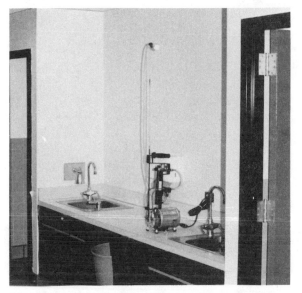

Monitoring pump set-up outside the enclosed room to detect asbestos being released from enclosure.

FIVE
MORAL MATTERS

You may ask what then will become of the fundamental principles of equity and fair play which our constitutions enshrine; and whether I seriously believe that unsupported they will serve merely as counsels of moderation. I do not think that anyone can say what will be left of those principles; I do not know whether they will serve only as counsels; but this much I think I do know — that a society so riven that the spirit of moderation is gone, no court can save; that a society where that spirit flourishes, no court need save; that in a society which evades its responsibility by thrusting upon the courts the nurture of that spirit, the spirit in the end will perish.

The late Billings Learned Hand, who wrote these words in 1942, served as a federal judge for 52 years. Much of his life was spent as chief judge of the Second Circuit, where he came to be so highly regarded that he often has been referred to as the "tenth justice" of the Supreme Court. In the quotation above (quoted at page 737 of Bartlett's *Familiar Quotations*, Little Brown and Company, Boston, 1980) he was not writing about asbestos, but his comments seem to fit perfectly the state of the law in the asbestos controversy today.

Like untested virtue, morality can scarcely be said to exist save in the face of difficult choices.

The choice of the word "morality" here is an intentional pun. The two most common meanings of the word "moral" are (a) "relating to or capable of making a distinction between right and wrong" and (b) "based upon general observation of people rather than on what is demonstrable, as in 'moral evidence.' "

Both senses are brought into play by the asbestos issue.

Is it right or wrong, for example, for government on the one hand to specify asbestos as a building material, to encourage domestic independence in the strategic material through subsidy and other means, and to make widespread use of the material itself in buildings, ships, draperies, clothing, and implements, and on the other hand to lay the blame for hazards attributable to the same material (whether or not the hazards are newly known, which by and large they are not) on those who manufactured the substance and those who followed the law by using it? And is not failure to choose the obviously right path a "moral" decision, in that it is a reaction to general observations of people rather than a reaction to what is demonstrable?

Bringing the issue closer to home and to the subject of this book, what is the moral duty of educators, who arguably are the preeminent social force dedicated to promotion of informed action over uninformed reaction?

The good news, as should be clear from Chapter 3, is that no educator need suffer guilt or remorse over creating or continuing an educational environment replete with asbestos. The bad news is that the law is not in accord with science on the subject, and some very hard decisions must be made.

As should be clear from Chapter 2, there is great personal risk to those in charge of schools and even greater risk to the school entities themselves, particularly in private schools, which can claim the cloak of government immunity in no state.

Our educational system can ill afford a multibillion-dollar added burden for which there is no demonstrable reward save avoiding legal liability. But the cost must be incurred.

An additional problem arises when one realizes that nonasbestos asbestiform fibers can be found in newer schools and that there is mounting evidence of hazards in the workplace for these similar to those for asbestos in the workplace. (See, for examples, "Studies of Fiberglass Workers Show Possible Link to Cancer," in the March 15, 1987, issue of the *New York Times* and "Health Studies Suggest Asbestos Substitutes also Pose Cancer Risk," May 12, 1987, issue of the *Wall Street Journal*.) If regulatory authorities make extrapolations for these similar to those made for asbestos, legal problems will arise for new schools, problems of such proportion as to dwarf the asbestos abatement legal problem.

A chapter is devoted to this short message because we think it is an important message. If our most basic institutions of learning cannot provide moral leadership, from whence will such hegemony come in a free society?

SIX
CONCLUSION

We have tried to accomplish two ambitious tasks in this book, one quite narrow, one very broad.

In our narrow, highly focused mission, we have tried to describe a perplexing dilemma facing thoughtful individuals involved in school management. On the one hand, there is great legal risk, personally and institutionally, to those in authority who fail to abate asbestos in school buildings. On the other hand, there is no scientific basis for abating; there are strong economic reasons not to engage in the wasteful exercise of abatement; and there are profound moral reasons not to seek restitution for abatement expense from those who supplied what in the past was legally mandated.

We have tried to present the basis for each element of the dilemma. That is, we have tried to explain in a rational and logical way the reasons for the irrational state of affairs, not by pointing fingers but by explaining the natural evolution of each course of independent events and phenomena that converge to the absurd situation of the present day.

Our dispassionate explanations have bearing on a much broader subject than asbestos, however. The phenomena about which we have written seem today to pervade many important aspects of U.S. life. Thousands of nearly parallel examples might be given. We offer one, by way of illustration.

Dr. Elizabeth B. Connell is professor of gynecology and obstetrics at Emory University School of Medicine in Atlanta. She has served on the Food and Drug Administration's Obstetrics and Gynecology Advisory Committee, the executive board of Planned Parenthood, and as an adviser to the United States Agency for International Development. She introduced a scholarly article in the May/June issue of MIT's *Technology Review* with the following words.

The United States has led the world in contraceptive research and development for many years. Americans have provided most of the basic scientific data, expertise, and manufacturing capability for contraceptive technologies now in use around the world. However, the United States is losing its leadership role in this area — with potentially disastrous consequences for women and men in this country and elsewhere.

The increasingly litigious climate in this country is one major reason for our technological slippage in this field. The growing number of lawsuits against companies that manufacture contraceptives has prompted many to withdraw products such as intrauterine devices (IUDs) from the marketplace. As a result, there are fewer contraceptive options available to Americans than there were a decade ago.

Fear of litigation has also discouraged companies from introducing safer and more convenient contraceptives to the domestic market, although they continue to test and sell new products abroad. It is particularly ironic that a number of excellent products developed by Americans, such as Depo-Provera (an injectable contraceptive) and the copper-bearing IUDs, are now available virtually everywhere in the world *except* in the United States.

This situation has been aggravated by widespread public misunderstanding about the risks and benefits of certain birth-control methods. This is particularly true of the pill, whose risks have been grossly exaggerated in proportion to its benefits. (Emphasis in original.)

Dr. Connell gives detailed explanations of the results of the foregoing phenomena. We have a teen-age pregnancy rate which is several times that of the rest of the developed world. To achieve sterility, older women suffer operations which impose high physical and psychological risk. Misunderstanding of probabilities and failure to address risk versus reward cause us to suffer under legislation imposing unreasonable standards of "safety" which only exacerbate the problem.

In short, while the asbestos in schools dilemma is absurd, unfortunately it is but one of many similar dilemmas facing this country.

The schools, arguably, are a principal source of molding future generations. The power of schools as a lobbying group is enormous. By and large, the voice of schools is respected. Surely the ingredients are present for schools to exercise leadership to achieve legislation which might dispel the asbestos dilemma and concurrently serve as a model for rationalizing many of the similar situations faced by others in this country.

APPENDIX A
House Report and Joint Explanatory Statement to the Asbestos Hazard Emergency Response Act of 1986

The Act has been reprinted in many places (including the Bureau of National Affairs' wonderful book, *Asbestos Abatement*) and is somewhat hard to read, as is the case with many statutes. A more enlightening document may be the House Report, which contains introductory background material and a section-by-section analysis of the Act.

The following is a verbatim rendering of portions of the House Report, which was adopted by both houses of Congress, and the Joint Explanatory Statement that accompanied the Act.

This legislation was introduced in the House on August 12, 1986, and in the Senate on September 10, 1986. It passed these bodies on October 1, 1986, and October 3, 1986, respectively, and was signed into law on October 22, 1986.

Footnotes are those of the authors.

HOUSE REPORT NO. 99-763
(Pages 14-34)

Purpose and Summary

H.R. 5073, the Asbestos Hazard Emergency Response Act of 1986, amends the Toxic Substances Control Act (TSCA) to deal with the problems caused by exposure to asbestos in the nation's public and private elementary and secondary school buildings. The actions taken by the Federal government to date do not give school officials sufficient guidance in identifying whether conditions in schools pose a hazard to human health and the environment and what to do about such hazards when they are identified.

Under H.R. 5073, the EPA (EPA) is required to promulgate regulations which prescribe proper inspection, response action and transport and disposal procedures. EPA is also required to establish a model contractor accreditation plan that the states must adopt, while the National Bureau of Standards is required to establish a laboratory accreditation program.

The legislation requires school districts to (1) inspect for asbestos-containing material, (2) prepare a management plan describing the response actions they will take regarding friable asbestos-containing materials, and (3) take the appropriate response actions where necessary to protect human health and the environment. The management plans must be submitted to the applicable state's Governor who may review and disapprove any plans that do not meet the standards established by the EPA regulations.

Furthermore, the bill amends the Asbestos School Hazard Abatement Act (ASHAA) to provide $100 million in additional funding over the next four years to assist schools in defraying the costs of inspecting for and abating asbestos. The $100 million authorization is funded by the creation of a trust fund into which all repayments of ASHAA loans will be made.

The bill also requires EPA to conduct a study which will assess the extent to which asbestos in public and commercial buildings poses a threat to human health. The study will assess whether public buildings should be subject to the same requirements that apply to schools and include recommendations that explicitly address the need to establish standards and regulate asbestos exposure in public and commercial buildings.

Background and Need for Legislation

EPA estimates that 15 million school children — almost one-third of the nation's school population — and 1.4 million school employees attend school and work in buildings which have asbestos materials. The best available figures indicate that about 31,000 school buildings contain at least some asbestos materials.

Asbestos is a known human carcinogen which can cause lung cancer, mesothelioma and asbestosis. Since children breathe five times faster than adults, they are much more susceptible to the effects of asbestos inhalation. For this reason, asbestos-containing material in school buildings can pose serious hazards for human health and the environment.

EPA first identified asbestos as a public health threat in the nation's schools in 1978. In May, 1982, EPA issued a final rule under TSCA requiring the inspection of all public and private elementary and secondary schools for asbestos-containing materials, take samples of all asbestos-containing materials found, analyze the samples, and maintain records of all inspection and sampling activities. The rule also requires those schools that have found friable asbestos-containing material to notify parents and employees of the location of the material and to post a standard notice in affected school areas. However, the rule does not require cleanup of the asbestos.

In August, 1984, the Congress passed the Asbestos School Hazard Abatement Act (ASHAA) which authorized $600 million in funding through fiscal year 1990 for asbestos response action grants and loans to school districts. To date, over $100 million has been appropriated for this program to assist schools in cleaning up friable asbestos-containing material. The loans are interest free and may be repaid over 20 years. Funding under the ASHAA school loan program is available only to school districts which can demonstrate financial need.

EPA distributed $45 million in grants and loans to school districts in June 1985 and distributed another $45 million this summer [1986]. Implementation of EPA's regulatory guidance and the ASHAA school loan program have not solved the problem of exposing children and school employees to asbestos in the nation's school buildings. Instead, the legacy of the rule in too many instances has been either no action or improper cleanup that has only exacerbated asbestos hazards.

EPA has not promulgated any regulations defining what constitutes a proper inspection. As a result, there is evidence that many inspections conducted to date have been inadequate. EPA also has yet to define the circumstances under which schools must respond to asbestos. Furthermore, EPA has not promulgated regulations telling school officials what actions should be taken to clean up asbestos when necessary to protect the health of school children and employees. Finally, EPA has not set standards by which the competence of asbestos abatement contractors can be evaluated.

In the absence of such standards, response action requirements and appropriate accreditation programs, school districts across the country have been repeatedly victimized by so-called "rip and skip" contractors. Improper cleanup has only resulted in increased exposure of school occupants to asbestos hazards.

Following a survey of its regional offices in 1985, EPA estimated that as much as 75 percent of all school cleanup work is being done improperly. Improper abatement work can be worse than no abatement work at all because more asbestos fibers are released into the air during the course of badly done cleanups than if the asbestos was not touched.

In 1984, the Service Employees International Union (SEIU) sued EPA to compel the agency to issue comprehensive regulations dealing with the asbestos problem in the nation's schools. *SEIU v. EPA*, No. 84-2790 (D.C.C.). Information developed in the SEIU lawsuit and provided to the Committee was of significant assistance in developing the legislation, which is in turn designed to provide the same relief sought in the lawsuit: issuance of adequate and appropriate EPA regulations regarding asbestos in schools.

H.R. 5073 creates a workable mechanism to rid school buildings of asbestos hazards to protect school children and employees from the dangers associated with exposure to airborne fibers of the mineral.

Hearing

The Committee's Subcommittee on Commerce, Transportation and Tourism held a hearing on the legislation on March 4, 1986. Testimony was received from Ms. Susan Vogt, Director, Asbestos Action Program, Office of Pesticides and Toxic Substances, U.S. EPA, Washington, D.C.; Mr. John Sweeney, President, Service Employees International Union, Washington, D.C.; Mr. Bob Robards, President, Service Employees International Union, Local 454, Newton, Massachusetts; Mr. Chet Poslusny, Chairman, Asbestos Committee, Mount Airy Elementary School, Mount Airy, Maryland; Ms. Annette Weaver, Past President, Brownsville Area Education Association, Brownsville, Pennsylvania; Mr. John Welch, President, Safe Buildings Alliance, Washington, D.C.; Mr. Anthony Natale, President, Duall Incorporated, Cherry Hill, New Jersey and Mr. C. B. Miller, Vice President, Petrin Corporation, Port Allen, Louisiana.

Written testimony and communication submitted for the record was received from Governor Toney Anaya (N.M.); Dr. William J. Nicholson, Associate Professor, Division of Environmental and Occupational Medicine, Mt. Sinai School of Medicine, New York, New York; and other professional and health organizations including the American Cancer Society, the American Institute of Architects, the American Lung Association, the American Federation of Teachers and the National Association of Asbestos Abatement Contractors.

Committee Consideration

On June 25, 1986, the Subcommittee on Commerce, Transportation and Tourism met in open session and ordered reported the bill H.R. 5073, without amendments, by a voice vote, a quorum being present. On July 29, 1986, the Committee met in open session and ordered reported the bill H.R. 5073, with a technical amendment, by voice vote, a quorum being present.

Committee Oversight Findings

Pursuant to clause 2(l)(3)(A) of rule XI of the Rules of the House of Representatives, the Subcommittee held oversight hearings and made findings that are reflected in the legislative report.

In October, 1985, the Environmental Protection Agency's (EPA) Inspector General completed a detailed review of the Agency's Asbestos-in-Schools Program in four regions — Boston, Philadelphia, Chicago and Los Angeles. These audits strongly criticized EPA's asbestos program by documenting a pattern of lax inspection and enforcement procedures and failures to distribute EPA guidance material, the only information the Federal government provides to assist schools in cleaning up asbestos.

The audits were critical of EPA's program for enforcing the requirements of the Agency's school asbestos inspection and notification rule. In addition, the audits stated that there are extensive delays in the issuance of enforcement actions and that most schools in the four regions, and presumably the entire nation, never even received a key guidance book published by the Agency in 1980. Finally, the audits questioned the ability of some of EPA's own inspectors to identify products containing friable asbestos.

Since EPA has issued only the inspection and notification rule, the audits did not even begin to address the serious problems caused by shoddy abatement work. In many cases, poor abatement work only serves to increase the asbestos hazard for school children and employees. An EPA survey of its regional officials in 1985 indicated that as many as a stunning 75 percent of all abatement projects were inadequately performed.

Although EPA has taken steps to improve its asbestos-in-schools outreach program, the fact remains that school officials have no regulations to follow to ensure proper cleanup of asbestos. Concern about inadequate inspection and clean-up activity had led the Committee to develop the Asbestos Hazard Emergency Response Act (H.R. 5073) in order to require EPA to promulgate regulations for inspection, cleanup and disposal of asbestos as well as a contractor accreditation program that the states must adopt. These regulations are needed to protect school children and employees from the hazards associated with exposure to asbestos.

Committee on Government Operations

Pursuant to clause 2(l)(3)(D) of rule XI of the Rules of the House of Representatives, no oversight findings have been submitted to the Committee by the Committee on Government Operations.

Committee Cost Estimate

In compliance with clause 7(a) of rule XIII of the Rules of the House of Representatives, the Committee believes that the cost incurred in carrying out H.R. 5073 would be a total of $100 million,[1] ranging from $11 million to $27 million per year for fiscal years 1987 through 1991.

U.S. Congress
Congressional Budget Office
Washington, D.C., August 1, 1986

Hon. John D. Dingell,
Chairman, Committee on Energy and Commerce,
U.S. House of Representatives, Washington, D.C.

Dear Mr. Chairman:

The Congressional Budget Office has prepared the attached cost estimate for H.R. 5073, the Asbestos Hazard Emergency Response Act of 1986.

If you wish further details on this estimate, we will be pleased to provide them.

With best wishes,
Sincerely,

Rudolph G. Penner,
Director, Congressional Budget Office, Cost Estimate

1. Bill number: H.R. 5073.
2. Bill title: Asbestos Hazard Emergency Response Act of 1986.
3. Bill status: As ordered reported by the House Committee on Energy and Commerce, July 29, 1986.
4. Bill purpose: H.R. 5073 would amend the Toxic Substances Control Act and the Asbestos School Hazard Abatement Act of 1984 to expand current federal and local responsibilities relating to asbestos hazards. The bill would direct the Environmental Protection Agency (EPA) to promulgate regulations for local school hazards abatement activities, including facility inspection, implementation of response actions, and periodic reinspection. The EPA would also be required to conduct a study of asbestos health risks and to develop a model contractor accreditation program for states.
5. Estimated cost to the Federal Government: (By fiscal years, in millions of dollars); 1987, authorization $30, outlays $11; 1988, $28, $27; 1989, $27, $27; 1990, $26, $26; 1991, -0-, $19.

The costs of this bill fall within budget function 300.

Basis of Estimate. For purposes of this estimate, CBO has assumed that H.R. 5073 will be enacted prior to the beginning of fiscal year 1987 and that the full amounts authorized will be appropriated for each fiscal year. Additional authorization levels have been estimated for EPA regulatory activities, including the promulgation of regulations under Section 2 and annual compliance monitoring. These costs are estimated to be about $5 million in 1987 and $3-4 million annually in subsequent years. Also, beginning in fiscal year 1989 the authorization level has been reduced to account for repayments on loans made under the bill. For the purposes of this estimate CBO has assumed that these repayments would reflect the same terms as those made under the 1984 act — repayments over 18 years, without interest, beginning two years after award. First year (1989) repayments are expected to be less than $1 million, growing to about $3 million by 1991.

Outlays for loans, grants, and administrative expenses have been estimated on the basis of historical spending patterns and information obtained from the EPA. Spending levels have been estimated assuming the same proportional split between loans and grants as for the current programs.

6. Estimated costs to State and local governments: H.R. 5073 would direct the EPA to impose stringent new requirements on local school authorities in their efforts to abate asbestos hazards. The bill would provide an additional $25 million a year to the schools to help them in carrying out their programs. These funds, which would be distributed on the basis of financial need, would supplement appropriations authorized under the 1984 act.

In addition to new local requirements, the bill would also expand the states' duties. As under current law, the states would continue to act in a middle-man capacity, collecting data and submissions from school authorities and conveying them to the EPA. In addition, the states would be required to review school management plans and establish contractor accreditation programs. No financial assistance is provided in the bill (or under existing law) for these purposes. At present, CBO has not completed its analysis of these requirements on state and local government budgets. This estimate will be submitted separately at a later date.[2]

7. Estimate comparison: None.

8. Previous CBO estimate: None.[3]

9. Estimate prepared by Deb Reis.

10. Estimate approved by James L. Blum, Assistant Director for Budget Analysis.

Inflationary Impact Statement

Pursuant to clause 2(l)(4) of rule XI of the Rules of the House of Representatives, the Committee makes the following statement with regard to the inflationary impact of the reported bill:

The Committee believes the passage and implementation of H.R. 5073 will have a significant and positive anti-inflationary impact.[4] The minimization, or elimination, of the diseases associated with exposure to asbestos will dramatically reduce, or eliminate, significant health costs at the least possible cost.[5] Furthermore, proper and timely response action implementation by accredited contractors according to the standards established as a result of H.R. 5073 will save substantial funds compared to the current situation. The use of accredited inspectors, consultants and laboratories according to the requirements of H.R. 5073 will ensure adequate work as well, allowing for additional savings compared to present practices related to the cleanup of asbestos in schools.[6]

Section by Section Analysis

Section 1: Short Title

The short title of the legislation is the Asbestos Hazard Emergency Response Act of 1986.

Section 2: Amendment to the Toxic Substances Control Act

This section amends the Toxic Substances Control Act by adding at the end the Asbestos Hazard Emergency Response Act of 1986 as Title II.

Section 201: Findings and Purpose

This section contains the findings that are the basis for the legislation. They include:

The Environmental Protection Agency's (EPA) rule on local educational agency inspection for, and the notification of, the presence of friable asbestos-containing material in school buildings includes neither standards for the proper identification of asbestos-containing material and appropriate response actions with respect to friable asbestos-containing material nor a requirement that response actions with respect to friable asbestos-containing material be carried out in a safe and complete manner. As a result of the lack of regulatory guidance from EPA, some schools have undertaken expensive projects without knowing if their actions are necessary or safe. Thus, exposure to asbestos continues to exist in schools and may actually have increased due to the lack of federal standards.

EPA's guidance document for responding to asbestos-containing materials in buildings is inadequate and too general and vague to provide sufficient guidance to local educational agencies for responding appropriately to asbestos and could lead to inappropriate responses in certain situations. Such guidance, as modified, is intended to be used only if EPA fails to promulgate regulations as required by this legislation.

Because of the absence of standards for building occupants in public and commercial buildings, persons in addition to the school population may be exposed daily to asbestos.

The section also states the purposes of the legislation, which include: (1) establishment of federal standards for identification of asbestos-containing material and the performance of response actions with respect to friable asbestos-containing material in the nation's schools; (2) mandating safe and complete periodic reinspection following response actions, where appropriate; and (3) requiring EPA to conduct a study that will assess whether asbestos in public and commercial buildings poses a danger to human health, including recommendations that address whether there is the need to establish standards with regard to asbestos in such buildings.

Section 202: Definitions

This section defines many of the terms used throughout this title. Among the most important definitions are the following:

The term "asbestos" means asbestiform varieties of chrysotile, crocidolite, amosite, anthophyllite, tremolite, or actinolite.

The term "asbestos-containing material" means any material which contains more than one percent asbestos by weight. Materials containing only trace elements of asbestos therefore would not be covered by the definition.

The term "friable asbestos-containing material" means any asbestos-containing material applied on walls, duct work, ceilings or any other part of a building which when dry may be crumbled, pulverized, or reduced to powder by hand pressure.

The term "response action" means methods to protect human health and the environment from asbestos-containing material. Such methods include methods described in chapters 3 and 5 of EPA's "Guidance for Controlling Asbestos-Containing Materials in Buildings," as in effect on March 31, 1986. Chapter 3 of the guidance document is entitled "Establishing a Special Operations and Maintenance Program." The chapter delineates work procedures and educational activities which are to be continued as long as the asbestos-containing material remains in a school building. Chapter 5 of the document, entitled "Abatement Methods: Characteristics and Recommended Work Practices," explains how to perform repair, removal, inclosure and encapsulation activities.

The legislation's definition of "response action" establishes the statutory standard which applies to actions taken and regulations issued under the Asbestos Hazard Emergency Response Act. That standard is the protection of human health and the environment. This standard is the same standard that applies to actions taken under the Resource Conservation and Recovery Act (RCRA) and is different from the "unreasonable risk" standard applicable under Section 6 of the Toxic Substances Control Act (TSCA).[7]

The "protection of human health and the environment" standard requires the agency to determine what actions are necessary to protect human health and environment from actual and potential asbestos hazards. Such hazards include actual or potential exposure to releases of asbestos that may cause adverse effects on human health or the environment. The agency must establish the levels of protection that are necessary to protect human health and the environment and the response actions that are necessary to achieve such levels.[8]

The primary human health effect of asbestos identified to date is the inhalation of airborne asbestos fibers. However, in determining whether the regulations issued under the Act meet the "protect human health and the environment" standard, the agency shall consider any other adverse health or environmental effects from asbestos brought to its attention during the rulemaking proceeding, including contamination of water supplies or the human food chain by asbestos.

The definition of response action under this provision includes a variety of methods identified in the EPA guidance document but would never include simply observing friable asbestos-containing materials visually without providing appropriate information and protection.

The term "EPA guidance document" means the EPA document titled "Guidance for Controlling Asbestos-containing Materials in Buildings" as modified by the agency after March 31, 1986.

The term "local educational agency" means the owner of any nonprofit, public or private, elementary or secondary school building and any local educational agency as defined in section 198 of the Elementary and Secondary School Act of 1965. This definition covers the same entities included under ASHAA — all public and private, elementary and secondary school authorities or owners. Vocational, for-profit educational facilities such as driver training and beautician schools are not included in this definition.

The term "school building" means any and all structures suitable for use in any and all phases of the instruction of students or the administration of educational and research programs, including classrooms, and such other school facilities as laboratories, libraries, gymnasiums, or school eating areas as well as any maintenance, storage or utility facilities essential to the operation of the structure. This definition also includes all school facilities now covered under ASHAA.

Section 203: EPA Regulations

This section requires the Administrator to promulgate regulations in seven areas within 360 days after the date of enactment of the Title. The Administrator is also required to issue an advanced notice of proposed rulemaking within 60 days of enactment and proposed regulations within 180 days after the date of enactment.

First the Administrator is required to promulgate regulations which prescribe the proper inspection procedures, including the use of accredited personnel, for determining whether asbestos-containing material is present in the nation's public and private elementary and secondary schools and require such inspections. The regulations shall exclude a school, or portion of a school, from the inspection requirement if an adequate inspection was completed before promulgation of the regulations.

Second, the Administrator is required to promulgate regulations which define what response actions must be taken in school buildings, using the least burdensome methods which adequately protect against adverse effects of asbestos.

In assessing the hazards caused by exposure to asbestos as it currently exists in schools, EPA should also consider the hazards likely to be posed by improper or inappropriate abatement activities, both to occupants of the school buildings and to the workers performing the response action work.

As noted in the above discussion of the legislation's definition of "response action," the statutory standard of "protection of human health and the environment"—the same standard that applies under RCRA—is applicable to actions taken under the Asbestos Hazard Emergency Response Act. The requirement that EPA use the least burdensome methods in defining appropriate response actions does not in any way affect this overriding standard.

Third, the Administrator is required to promulgate regulations which define and require the appropriate response action in school buildings when either (1) the friable asbestos-containing material or its covering is damaged, deteriorated or delaminated or (2) the friable asbestos-containing material is in an area regularly used by building occupants, there is a reasonable likelihood the material will become damaged, deteriorated or delaminated and there is a reasonable likelihood that the material when damaged, deteriorated or delaminated would require a response action.

This provision of the legislation establishes a statutory definition of the minimum circumstances which, when they exist in a school building, must be covered by the agency's regulations requiring that appropriate action be taken. That is, the regulations must require response actions in the circumstances identified under section 203(d).

Those circumstances cover two distinct types of situations. The first is when friable asbestos-containing material or the covering on such material is damaged, deteriorated or delaminated. This type of situation presents the concern that asbestos fibers have been or will be released, as a result of the damage, deterioration or delamination.

The second type of situation involves circumstances where the asbestos-containing material is not yet damaged, deteriorated or delaminated. If such undamaged material is located in an area which is regularly (i.e. routinely) used by building occupants, and the conditions of such use present a reasonable likelihood that the material will become damaged, deteriorated or delaminated, the regulations must require appropriate response actions. In determining the reasonable likelihood of damage, deterioration or delamination and defining what response actions shall be taken, the agency shall apply the same criteria it uses in determining what response actions must be taken in the first type of situation, when the material is already so damaged. These criteria would involve an assessment of the scope and severity of the potential damage, deterioration and delamination and its impact on human health and the environment, although the response action required by the agency might be geared to preventing such damage and therefore might be different than the response action required after such damage has occurred.

The provision defining circumstances where there is a reasonable likelihood of potential damage is applicable to areas within a building which any or all building occupants routinely use and would include, in addition to areas regularly used by teachers, children and administrative personnel, areas regularly or routinely used by maintenance personnel such as boiler and utility rooms, storage sites, ventilation systems or lighting systems.

The determination of whether there is a "reasonable likelihood" that the material will become damaged, deteriorated or delaminated will involve an assessment that the present conditions of use raise the real possibility that such damage will occur. For example, if undamaged asbestos-containing material is located in a gymnasium ceiling where children play basketball, and therefore there is a real possibility that the collision of a basketball with the ceiling may damage such material, a reasonable likelihood would exist.

In promulgating these regulations, the Administrator must consider the value of various technologies intended to improve the decision-making process regarding response actions and the quality of the work deemed necessary, including air monitoring and chemical removal encapsulants. Although this field is the subject of numerous possible technological advances, the legislation identifies two technologies as being worth mentioning, air monitoring and chemical removal encapsulation. Air monitoring is concerned with measuring the asbestos-in-air concentration. This technology could potentially be valuable in assessing the need for and timing of abatement action, although problems associated with using the technology to identify peak, unpredictable exposures to asbestos remain to be resolved. The second technology is significant in the potential it offers in securely and economically affording protection once the hazard has been measured and identified.

Fourth, the Administrator is required to promulgate regulations establishing procedures for the safe and effective implementation of response actions and, where appropriate, for the determination of when response action is completed in school buildings. These regulations must include standards for the protection and education of both workers and building occupants for the three phases of activity: (1) inspection; (2) response action; and (3) post-response action, including any periodic reinspection of asbestos-containing material and long-term surveillance activity. Because school maintenance workers performing operations and maintenance activities are more likely to be exposed to asbestos hazards, the local educational agency must emphasize health and safety rules for such persons and activities.

Fifth, the Administrator is required to promulgate regulations which require the implementation of an operation and maintenance and repair program as described in chapter 3 of the EPA guidance document for all friable asbestos-containing materials in schools.

Sixth, the Administrator is required to promulgate regulations governing the transport and disposal of asbestos which protect human health and the environment, again the same standard that applies under RCRA.

Seventh, the Administrator is required to promulgate regulations which require each local educational agency to develop management plans for school buildings under its authority and to begin implementation of the plan within 900 days of enactment and to complete implementation in a timely fashion.

The potential severity of the hazards posed by asbestos-containing materials underscores the need for prompt action by the schools once EPA has issued appropriate regulations. The 900-day deadline for management plans requires not only that the schools develop such plans, but also that they begin implementing them within the deadline and complete implementation in a timely fashion. When asbestos remains in schools, long-term operation and maintenance activity is necessary. The requirement that the local educational agency begin implementation applies to each of the school buildings within the agency's control. The activities required and the timing of their implementation will vary depending upon the severity of the hazards posed by the asbestos-containing materials found in each school. However, the grave nature of the adverse health and environmental effects caused by asbestos mandates that appropriate action be taken and completed in all affected school buildings as expeditiously as possible.

The regulations shall require that each management plan contain several elements, wherever relevant to a school building. These elements include:

a statement describing inspections done before enactment;

a description of the results of any inspection conducted after enactment, pursuant to the regulations promulgated by the Administrator;

a schedule for and description of response actions to be conducted;

a description of any asbestos-containing material for which no response action has already been taken;

a plan for periodic reinspection, long-term surveillance activities and operation and maintenance activities;

a statement that all inspectors, consultants and contractors are accredited;

a laboratory accreditation statement;

an evaluation of necessary resources to implement the plan.

A local educational agency which has carried out its stated response actions must attach a warning label to any asbestos-containing material or friable asbestos-containing material still in routine maintenance areas of the school. The label shall read: CAUTION: ASBESTOS. HAZARDOUS. DO NOT DISTURB WITHOUT PROPER TRAINING AND EQUIPMENT.

This section also requires that a copy of the management plan be made available in the administrative offices of the local educational agency for inspection by the public, including teachers, other school personnel and parents.

The management plan must also be submitted to the State Governor for review.

The section specifically clarifies that any changes to the initial regulations issued by the agency must also comply with the general standard of protection of human health and the environment that applies to such initial regulations, and that such changes must also be promulgated in accordance with section 553 of the Administrative Procedures Act.

Section 204: Requirements if EPA Fails to Promulgate Regulations[9]

This section states that if the Administrator fails to promulgate regulations within the prescribed time period, each local educational agency will be required to do the following (in accordance with the most current EPA guidance document): conduct an inspection within 540 days of enactment, using accredited personnel unless an inspection carried out prior to enactment meets the requirements of this section; (2) develop and begin carrying out within 720 days of enactment an operation and maintenance plan for all friable asbestos-containing material in each school building; (3) develop a management plan responding to all friable asbestos-containing material in each school building under its authority and submit the plan to the Governor within 810 days after enactment; (4) begin implementation of the plan within 900 days after enactment and complete the implementation in a timely fashion; and (5) provide for the transportation and disposal of asbestos in accordance with the most recent version of EPA's "Asbestos Waste Management Guidance" (or any successor to the document). The local educational agency is also required to protect building occupants during each phase of response action activity. Because school maintenance workers performing operations and maintenance activities are more likely to be exposed to asbestos hazards, the local educational agency must emphasize health and safety rules for such persons and activities.

The management plan the local educational agencies develop must include the elements listed in section 203, including an inspection statement describing any inspections and other actions undertaken by the local educational agencies prior to enactment.

This section establishes the "hammer" requirements that shall be implemented if EPA fails to promulgate regulations under section 203 within 360 days after enactment. However, because a central purpose of the legislation is to ensure that comprehensive, objective regulations are promulgated to replace the current guidance that is both inadequate and leads to inappropriate responses, a number of provisions are included in the hammer to enhance the certainty that regulations defining appropriate response actions will take effect before local educational agencies are required to begin implementing the management plan 900 days after enactment.

Accordingly, section 204 provides for the "hammer" actions to be taken in successive incremental steps. Within 540 days, the inspection with respect to asbestos-containing material in a school building is to be conducted in accordance with EPA's most current guidance document. The regulations shall exclude a school, or portion of a school, from the inspection requirement if an adequate inspection was completed before promulgation of the regulations. The operation and maintenance plan is to be developed and implementation begun within 720 days.

If EPA has failed to promulgate regulations under section 203 within 810 days after enactment, local educational agencies shall develop and submit to the affected state Governor their management plans for responding to friable asbestos-containing material and based upon the most current guidance document of EPA. Implementation of the management plans shall begin within 900 days after the date of enactment.

To further enhance the likelihood that regulations will be adopted prior to implementation of management plans, though, section 207(g) provides for an immediate appeal in the event that EPA fails to meet one of the interim dates or the final date for carrying out the rulemaking process, and the federal court with jurisdiction is authorized to take into account the balance of the schedule when any date for action in the rulemaking is not met. In addition, the court is authorized to extend the effective date of the "hammer" provision by up to six months, if this will result in response actions being taken pursuant to regulations promulgated under section 203 rather than pursuant to EPA's guidance. However, this extension may not be granted in orders issued on dates following 720 days after enactment of this title.

The section also contains a standard following the completion of response actions other than operation and maintenance activities which must be met before areas that have undergone response actions can be reoccupied. The standard is that ambient interior concentrations shall not exceed ambient exterior concentration.[10] In the absence of reliable measurements, the ambient exterior concentration shall be less than 0.003 fibers per cubic centimeter if a scanning electron microscope (SEM) is used and 0.005 fibers per cubic centimeter if a transmission electron microscope (TEM) is used.

The legislation establishes that phase contrast microscopy (PCM) should not be used to analyze air samples of asbestos in school buildings. PCM is an inadequate tool for use in public and commercial buildings because of its inability to distinguish asbestos fibers from other materials and to detect the most microscopic fibers. The legislation mandates the use of electron microscopy — either scanning or transmission. Electron microscopy is superior to PCM because it can distinguish asbestos fibers from other materials and it can detect the short, thin fibers likely to be airborne in school buildings.[11]

While SEM is not able to detect fibers as small as those that TEM can detect, it is an adequate tool for use in analyzing air samples for asbestos in school buildings. SEM is more available, easier to use, and less expensive than TEM. The only disadvantage of SEM is that a protocol has yet to be developed for this technology. The Congress expects a protocol to be developed by the National Bureau of Standards before the end of 1986.[12]

TEM is clearly the best available technology. Although at this point, TEM is difficult to use, expensive and not readily available, the cost and availability problems associated with TEM, and to a lesser extent SEM, will likely be eased as the market responds to the needs of contractors who must use electron microscopy to meet the reoccupancy standard in this section.

The section also states that a copy of the management plan must be made publicly available in the administrative offices of the local educational agency for inspection by the public including parents, teachers and other school personnel.

Section 205: State Governor Review

This sections states that within 360 days after the date of enactment of this title, the Governor of each state shall notify local educational agencies of where to submit their management plans and may establish administrative procedures for reviewing the management plans submitted by each local educational agency. Within 720 days after enactment (or 810 days if section 204 is in effect), the local educational agency must submit its management plan to the Governor of its State.

This section states that the Governor may disapprove a management plan within 90 days after it is received if the plan does not assure that accredited contractors will be used, does not conform to the regulations promulgated by the Administrator (or section 204 if the Administrator does not act) or does not contain a response action schedule which is both timely and reasonable. If the Governor disapproves a plan, he shall explain in writing to the local educational agency the reasons why the plan was disapproved and the changes that need to be made. The local educational agency must revise the plan within 30 days after receiving the Governor's explanation, although the Governor may extend by up to 90 days the time the local educational agency has to revise the plan.[13]

A key element of the Governor's review, and an essential factor in any decision regarding the acceptability of a management plan, is whether the plan establishes a reasonably timely and expeditious schedule for the completion of response actions. The legislation does not establish any uniform national schedule for response actions because circumstances affecting the timing of such actions in each individual school district will vary. Instead, one of the most important functions of the State Governor review is to ensure that such plans contain reasonable schedules.

Section 206: Contractor and Laboratory Accreditation

This section states that a person may not inspect for asbestos-containing material in a school, prepare a management plan for a local educational agency or conduct a response action, other than operation and maintenance activities, in a school unless the person is accredited either by a state or an EPA approved training course.

Within 180 days after enactment, the EPA Administrator in consultation with affected organizations must develop a model contractor accreditation plan for states to accredit persons who inspect schools for asbestos-containing material, persons who prepare management plans for local educational agencies and persons who carry out response actions other than operation and maintenance activities in schools. The plan must provide for mandatory pass/fail testing to determine competence and for continuing education of those accredited.[14]

Within 180 days after commencement of the first regular session of state legislatures following establishment of the model plan, states shall adopt a contractor accreditation plan at least as stringent as the one developed by the Administrator.

The section also provides for conferring automatic accreditation on certain categories of people who took EPA-approved training courses prior to the date of enactment.

This section also states that within 180 days after the date of enactment of this title, the Secretary of Commerce, acting through the National Bureau of Standards and in consultation with affected organizations, shall develop an accreditation program for laboratories that analyze either air samples of asbestos or bulk samples of asbestos-containing material for local educational agencies.[15]

This section mandates that any local educational agency applying for ASHAA funds for work done after enactment is not eligible for financial assistance unless the local educational agency uses persons accredited either by a state or by an EPA-approved training course and laboratories accredited under the program established by the Secretary of Commerce.

Section 207: Enforcement

This section states that any local educational agencies are liable for civil penalties not to exceed $5,000 a day for the following types of violations: (1) failure to conduct an inspection; (2) knowing submission of false information to the Governor or including false information in any management plan; or (3) failure to prepare and implement a management plan in a timely fashion as required either under EPA regulations or under the fallback procedures and standards established by the legislation if EPA does not issue such regulations. Only the U.S. Attorney General or the Attorney General from the affected State may bring an action to collect any such penalty. Any such penalty shall be ordered by the court to be returned to the local educational agency for purposes of complying with this title.

This section also states that if a local educational agency fails to conduct an inspection, fails to prepare a management plan, or fails to complete implementation of the management plan, then the U.S. or state Attorney General may seek injunctive relief requiring the local educational agency to comply with such requirements. In any such compliance action, the EPA Administrator, if not a party, may intervene as a matter of right. The court may award costs of the suit and reasonable fees for attorneys if the court determines that such an award is appropriate.

The section states that the local educational agencies shall be subject to penalties and enforcement actions if there is a failure to meet, in a timely fashion, regulatory or statutory requirements in any of the school buildings subject to the control of the agency.

The section provides that if the U.S. or affected state Attorney General has commenced and is diligently pursuing an enforcement action then no other person may bring an action. Furthermore, no action may be brought before the expiration of 60 days after the plaintiff has notified the Administrator and the local education agency of the alleged lack of compliance.

In fashioning any relief in a compliance action, the court may consider the degree of the hazard posed by the asbestos and the resources available to the local educational agency to conduct any action the court orders it to take.

This provision of the legislation does not affect the equitable powers of the courts to fashion appropriate relief, but merely suggests those specific facts which the courts may wish to consider in determining how to structure such relief. Where there is a serious hazard and the need for rapid cleanup, the protection of human health and the environment should be the paramount consideration of the courts.

This section also provides for the filing of citizens' complaints. Any citizen may file a complaint with the Administrator or the affected State Governor regarding asbestos in a school building. Following receipt of the complaint, the Administrator or Governor is required to investigate, respond to the citizen in a reasonable period of time, and turn any information about possible violations over to the appropriate law enforcement authorities.

This sections states that any person may commence a civil action against the Administrator to compel the Administrator to meet the deadlines established in section 203 for issuing advanced notices of proposed rulemaking, proposed regulations and final regulations.

The statute is deliberately broad with respect to standing to sue. In this respect, it parallels the citizen suits provision found in the Clean Air Act and TSCA. However, unlike the citizen suits provisions found in other sections of TSCA, this section of the bill does not establish the requirements of notice to the Administrator prior to the filing of an action alleging its failure to meet the deadlines established in section 203. Notice to the Administrator is provided by section 203, which sets forth a precise mandated timetable for the issuance of an advance notice of proposed rulemaking, proposed regulations and promulgated regulations.

Any civil action shall be brought in the district court for the District of Columbia. If the court finds the Administrator to be in violation of any of the deadlines in section 203, the court shall order the Administrator to comply with a court-determined schedule. In other words, as soon as EPA misses one deadline, and that failure to comply with a statutory mandate is brought to the attention of a court, any relief ordered by the court shall include a court-ordered schedule for compliance with all subsequent deadlines included in the legislation.

The section gives the courts limited discretion to extend any statutory deadline, which has not already occurred as of the date of the court order, for a period not to exceed six months, if the court-ordered schedule will result in final promulgation of all regulations within the six month extension. Such extensions may not be granted in orders issued on dates following 720 days after enactment of this title.

Section 208: Emergency Authority

This section states that whenever the presence of airborne asbestos or friable asbestos-containing material in a school poses an immediate and significant hazard to human health or the environment and the local educational agency is not taking sufficient action to respond to the hazard, the Administrator or Governor of a state is authorized to act to protect human health or the environment and to recover the costs of any action taken. The Governor must notify EPA 40 days in advance of any action, except evacuation. The Governor may act at the end of the period only if the Administrator has not taken emergency action.

Immediate and significant hazards may involve actual or potential releases of asbestos fibers where the gravity of the situation necessitates intervention because of the lack of sufficient response to such hazard.

This section also states that upon receiving evidence that the presence of asbestos in a school poses an immediate and significant hazard to human health or the environment, the Administrator may request the U.S. Attorney General to bring suit or the Governor of a state may bring suit in the appropriate federal district court to secure the necessary relief to respond to such hazard. Liability for the relief sought shall be determined under the laws of the state in which the response will occur.

Section 209: State and Federal Law

This section states that other than section 210 nothing in this title shall be construed as preempting a state from establishing any additional liability or more stringent requirements with respect to asbestos in schools. It adds that the legislation does not affect any litigation asserting a claim for damages or other relief related to asbestos in buildings other than actions brought to enforce this title.

The section also states that other than section 210 no requirement of this title, no regulation promulgated under this title, and no order issued under this title may be introduced as evidence, in any action relating to asbestos other than an action brought to enforce this title. However, nothing in this section shall prohibit introduction as evidence of conditions discovered, work performed, or costs incurred under the requirements of this title.

The purpose of this section is to neutralize the effect of the legislation on any damage or personal injury suits filed under state law. The goal of the legislation is to accomplish the rapid, safe, effective and appropriate responses to asbestos in schools, not to influence in either the plaintiff's or the defendant's favor the disposition of any state product liability cases. Moreover, no new cause of action is created under this legislation.

At the same time, the section explicitly permits introduction into evidence in state law proceedings of factual information regarding conditions discovered and work performed as a direct result of the new legislative requirements. Examples of such factual information might include inspection reports, photographs of school conditions, laboratory samples and analysis, management plans, and bills from contractors for work performed.

The prohibition on introduction into evidence of requirements, regulations or orders does not preclude the impeachment of testimony that there are no such federal regulations, requirements, or orders. For example, if a party states that there are no federal regulations requiring response actions, its opponent may introduce such regulations to rebut such statements.

Section 210: Asbestos Contractors and Local Educational Agencies

This section states that when any activity required by this title is carried out in conformance with such requirements by an accredited contractor or local educational agency, damages for personal injury or property damage resulting from these activities may not be recovered from such contractor or agency unless the damages are caused by actions which are negligent, grossly negligent, or constitute intentional misconduct. An accredited contractor or local educational agency which is a defendant in such action may not be held jointly liable but may be held severally liable.

This provision extends only to activities carried out as a direct result of, in compliance with, the requirements of the legislation and regulations issued under it and does not extend to liability arising from any other activities of either the contractor or the local educational agency, including acts or omissions not required by the legislation.

Section 211: Public Protection

This section mandates that no person can be discriminated against by a state or local educational agency for providing information relating to a potential violation of this title to any other person, including to a State or to the Federal Government.

Section 212: Asbestos Ombudsman

This section requires the Administrator to appoint an Asbestos Ombudsman who will be responsible for receiving complaints, grievances and requests for information, rendering assistance with respect to complaints, grievances and requests received and making recommendations to the Administrator that the Ombudsman considers appropriate.

Section 213: EPA Study of Asbestos-Containing Material in Public Buildings

This section requires EPA to conduct and submit to Congress within 360 days of enactment of this title a study which will (1) assess whether asbestos-containing materials in public and commercial buildings pose a danger to human health, (2) report whether public and commercial buildings should be subject to the same requirements that apply to schools, and (3) include recommendations that explicitly address whether there is the need to establish standards and regulate asbestos exposure in public and commercial buildings.[16]

By including this study in the legislation, as opposed to prescribing a legislative course of action, the Committee is not prejudging the broader issue of whether the presence of asbestos-containing materials in public and commercial buildings requires any federal response. The legislation is designed to address a problem that involves our nation's schools. It is a specifically focused bill designed to address a clearly identified problem that has been the subject of intense scrutiny and study for several years. The study of asbestos-related problems involving buildings other than schools will ensure that these problems receive the same level of scrutiny and study.

Upon further analysis and completion of the study mandated in section 213 of this bill, the EPA may conclude that the same federal response to public buildings is necessary, that no federal response is necessary or that a very different federal response is appropriate in dealing with the broader question of asbestos-containing materials that may be present in public and commercial buildings.

Section 214: Transition Rules

This section states that any regulation promulgated by EPA under Title I which is inconsistent with this title shall no longer be in effect once this title is enacted. The provision should be narrowly construed. Only regulations which contradict or undermine specific provisions of the legislation are affected.

This section further states that any enforcement action relating to an EPA regulation on asbestos that is pending in court at the time of enactment of this title shall not be affected by this title.

Section 3: Technical and Conforming Amendments

This section contains the technical and conforming amendments necessary to conform this title to the Asbestos School Hazard Abatement Act and the Toxic Substances Control Act.

Section 4: Authorization

This section states that the Asbestos School Hazard Abatement Act of 1984 (ASHAA) is amended by increasing the authorization for each fiscal year, 1987 through 1990, by $25 million from $100 million to $125 million per year. This authorization is off-budget because no new funds are required. Instead, the funds for this authorization will come from the Asbestos Trust Fund created in section 5.

This section also allows the Administrator to provide not more than 10 percent of the fiscal year 1988 ASHAA appropriation to local educational agencies to carry out inspections and to prepare management plans. The Administrator shall take into account the financial need of the local educational agency in determining which local educational agencies receive the funds.

Section 5: Asbestos Trust Fund

This section creates a trust fund in the United States Treasury to be known as the "Asbestos Trust Fund." On or after January 1, 1987, all repayments to the Treasury of loans made under section 505 of the Asbestos School Hazard Abatement Act shall be transferred to the trust fund. Transfers totalling the amounts of the repayments shall be made at least monthly from the Treasury to the trust fund.

The Secretary of the Treasury shall invest portions of the trust fund that are not, in his judgment, required to meet current withdrawals from the trust fund. Such investments may be made only in interest-bearing obligations of the United States. Any obligation of the trust fund may be sold by the Secretary of the Treasury at the market price. The interest and proceeds from the sale and redemption of any obligations held in the trust fund shall be credited to the trust fund.

The section also states that the Secretary of the Treasury has the responsibility to hold the trust fund and annually report to the Congress on the financial condition and the result of the operations of the trust fund during the preceding fiscal year and on its condition and operation during the next five fiscal years.

Amounts in the trust fund are only available for carrying out the Assistance Program under section 505 of the Asbestos School Hazard Abatement Act.

The section also states the funds are authorized as repayable advances to the trust fund for $25 million for each fiscal year, 1987 through 1990. Advances from the trust fund shall be made when the Secretary of the Treasury determines that such funds are available. The advance shall be repaid with interest (at a sale determined by the Secretary of the Treasury to be equal to the current average market yield and outstanding marketable obligations of the United States to the Treasury general fund).

The Asbestos Trust Fund will be no cost to the Federal government and yet will allow for an additional $100 million authorization for ASHAA. Repayments to the U.S. Treasury by local educational agencies for loans made under the ASHAA will be transferred to the Trust Fund. These repayments will generate the increased $100 million authorization. Since local educational agencies have 20 years to repay the interest-free loan, the funds will not be immediately available. As a result, the Trust Fund will advance the money for the increased fiscal year 1987 through 1990 authorizations. The advances will be repaid by the Trust Fund with interest to the U.S. Treasury, thus making the Trust Fund cost-free. The advances can be repaid with interest because the Trust Fund will take in substantially more than the increased authorization will cost, given the current ASHAA authorization.

JOINT EXPLANATORY STATEMENT ON COMPROMISE AGREEMENT ON H.R. 5073

(found at 132 *Congressional Record* S 15065, October 3, 1986)

The legislation requires the Administrator to promulgate regulations which define what "response actions" must be taken in school buildings, using the least burdensome methods which protect human health and the environment.

The statutory standard of "protection of human health and the environment" is the same standard that applies under the Resource Conservation and Recovery Act (RCRA) and is different from the "unreasonable risk" standard applicable under section 6 of the Toxic Substances Control Act (TSCA).

The "protection of human health and the environment" standard requires the agency to determine what actions will protect human health and the environment from actual or potential asbestos hazards. Such hazards include actual or potential exposure to releases of asbestos that may cause adverse effects on human health or the environment. The "protect human health and the environment" standard does not require EPA to establish a quantitative relationship between the physical characteristics of the asbestos-containing materials (e.g., their condition or location) and the health risks which may be posed by exposure to airborne asbestos fibers. The legislation does not intend that the agency be either required to or prohibited from using such technologies as air monitoring in meeting the standard. It does not require or prohibit the agency from developing a model relating physical characteristics of the material to ambient fiber levels. The legislation also does not require or prohibit the agency from conducting a quantitative risk assessment relating ambient fiber levels to a particular amount of actual or potential health risks.

The requirement that EPA use the "least burdensome methods" in defining appropriate response actions does not in any way affect the overriding health standard that applies to the regulations — i.e., "protection of human health and the environment." Any method, or response action, selected by the agency must meet this overriding health standard. Once EPA determines the set of response actions that will meet the standard, the agency should make a separate determination of what constitutes the "least burdensome" approach.

The legislation recognizes that local circumstances — including how a specific school uses the building at issue, and the long-and short-term costs posed by the various options in the context of the local situation — could affect EPA's selection of the "least burdensome" methods.

The legislation does not in any way affect the prerogative of local educational agencies to go further or do more work, than the least burdensome methods selected by the EPA regulations.

The legislation establishes four categories of circumstances in which EPA must prescribe, by regulation, appropriate response actions for friable asbestos-containing material. The four circumstances are: (1) situations where friable asbestos-containing material is damaged, deteriorated or delaminated; (2) situations where friable asbestos-containing material is "significantly" damaged, deteriorated or delaminated; (3) situations where there is a potential (i.e., "reasonable likelihood") that the material will become damaged, deteriorated or delaminated in specified areas of the school; and (4) situations where there is a potential that the material will become "significantly" damaged, deteriorated or delaminated in such areas.

The Administrator must describe appropriate response actions in "at least" these four circumstances. The language means that, at a minimum, the EPA regulations must cover these circumstances by requiring implementation of response actions described for each of these circumstances. This language is derived from the Senate bill (S. 2083) which required prescription of response action, "at a minimum" in such circumstances. The "at least" language in the final legislation carries out the same statutory intent.

For the first circumstance, where the asbestos has already become damaged, deteriorated or delaminated, "response actions" include methods identified in Chapters 3 and 5 of the EPA Guidance Document. Chapter 3 sets forth operations and maintenance methods, including minor repair. Chapter 5 includes enclosure, encapsulation, removal and relatively major repairs. Chapter 3 methods can never be used when asbestos has become "significantly" damaged, deteriorated or delaminated, although such methods remain an option when the asbestos is only damaged, deteriorated or delaminated.

The legislation contemplates that new technologies may be developed that will expand the universe of methods contained in both Chapters 3 and 5.a. If such technologies do become available, EPA should include them in its regulations, so long as the new technologies — or methods — protect human health and the environment. By referencing Chapters 3 and 5, the legislation establishes a floor of appropriate response actions but does not freeze the development of new, more protective and more cost-effective technologies to accomplish the overall goal of meeting the health standard in the legislation.

For the third and fourth circumstances, where asbestos has not yet become damaged, deteriorated or delaminated, or where there is a "reasonable likelihood" it will become damaged, deteriorated or delaminated, the legislation requires that EPA prescribe "preventive" measures that will either prevent the likelihood of damage, deterioration and delamination or will otherwise protect human health and the environment.

For example, a school gymnasium used for basketball practice contains a ceiling composed of friable asbestos-containing material. The ceiling is not yet damaged, deteriorated or delaminated, but there is a "reasonable likelihood" it will become so as the school year progresses and basketballs are constantly thrown against it. The school could "prevent" damage by a variety of methods, including covering the ceiling with a net to prevent the balls from striking it or using another facility for basketball practice. The EPA regulations should develop such preventive methods fully and prescribe them for all potential damage situations.

Once again, preventive measures can include either methods to prevent damage or methods (such as closing the room) which will prevent adverse health effects as a result of exposure to airborne asbestos fibers. If damage, deterioration, or delamination is prevented, the minimal circumstances established by the legislation are never created. If damage, deterioration or delamination cannot be prevented, but other measures will protect human health and the environment, such methods would meet the statutory standard.

Section 204 contains a standard following the completion of response actions other than operation and maintenance activities which must be met before areas that have undergone response actions can be reoccupied. The section mandates that only electron microscopy can be used to analyze air samples to ensure that the standard has been met. The section establishes that phase contrast microscopy should not be used because it is an inadequate tool in that it cannot distinguish asbestos from other materials nor can it detect the most microscopic fibers.

The Congress recognizes that transmission electron microscopy is superior to scanning electron microscopy. However, at this point, transmission microscopy is expensive and not readily available. But these problems with transmission microscopy will likely be eased as the market responds to the needs of contractors who must use electron microscopy to meet the reoccupancy standard.

The new Title II of TSCA is subject to the provisions of Sections 15, 16, 19 and 20 of TSCA, except where Title II specifically provides otherwise. These exceptions include reduced civil penalty limits for certain infractions by local education agencies, requirements for channeling certain penalty payments back to local education agencies, specific factors to be used in determining the amount of a civil penalty against local education agencies, and deletion of the 60-day notice requirement with respect to citizens' civil actions against the Administrator for failure to meet a statutory deadline in section 203. Except as specifically provided in Title II, the usual TSCA provisions related to administrative civil penalties, maximum penalties and citizens' suits remain unchanged and may be used with regard to actions required by Title II.

NOTES

1. The correct base number is on the order of well over $50 billion ($5.0x10^{10}$), not $100 million ($1.0x10^8$). That is, the actual base "cost" would be roughly 500 times the estimate. The Committee Report states at the

outset that an estimated 15 million schoolchildren are involved. The average square footage occupied by a school child in Virginia, for example, a state not known to be profligate in providing for students, is 155 square feet (see Comm. of Va. Sptd. Memo #226, November 1986). While there are no data on the average cost of abatement, the range is $5.25 to $35 per square foot. An educated guess at the average might be roughly $23 per square foot. This would give an estimated total cost of over $53 billion plus whatever administrative costs may be involved in inspection, procurement, and the like. To this base cost one must add the cost of the contractor and laboratory regulatory scheme mandated by the Act and the periodic reinspection program.

2. At this writing we have been unable to locate any such estimates. However, see *id.*

3. In summary, no cost-benefit analysis was done in preparation for any of the prior acts of Congress on this subject and none was done prior to passage of H.R. 5073. Nor, to our knowledge, has any been done to date.

4. To the extent that productivity is in any way tied to inflation, this statement would appear to be difficult to support.

5. As explained in detail in the text of this book, the "risks" associated with asbestos in buildings in theory are so small as to be difficult to measure, and in fact there has never been an instance of such a risk materializing. The cost versus benefit implications of this sentence, therefore, are difficult to comprehend.

6. Licensing of abatement contractors, inspectors, consultants, and laboratories may or may not be desirable, but the reasons given here are either inaccurate or irrelevant. Creating a regulatory bureaucracy (or, in this case, 50 bureaucracies plus federal oversight) does not save money; it costs money. The benefits of licensing are that the customer is relieved of performing judgment and due diligence functions that otherwise would be done directly by the customer or indirectly through bonding. The detriment is that regulation is very expensive and the customer bears the cost. Bonding usually will be required in any event, so the customer will pay twice. In addition, regulation tends to serve as a barrier to entry into the business, in that one cannot become licensed without experience and one cannot obtain experience without a license. Limitations to entry decrease competition and thereby raise prices still further.

7. Actually, in addition to the RCRA standard ("protection of human health and the environment"), there are at least ten different federal standards having to do with allegedly toxic substances: (1) "zero risk," (2) "to the extent feasible," (3) "de minimis," (4) "natural standard," (5) "unreasonable risks," (6) "significant risk," (7) "adequate margin of safety," (8) "reasonable, necessary, or appropriate," (9) "ample margin of safety," and (10) "as low as reasonably achievable." Each of these has been amplified

by statute, regulation, and judicial interpretation as a separate and distinct standard. The differences include whether and the extent to which cost and benefit are to be compared, technical feasibility, and whether risk is to be assessed from a societal or weakest individual perspective. An excellent comparison of these standards may be found in the article of Ricci and Cox, cited in the bibliography.

8. A joint statement of the House and Senate has expanded upon the required standard. The Joint Statement is reprinted at the end of this Report.

9. The proposed regulations were issued in a timely fashion and are contained in this book. There is no reason to believe the final regulations will not be adopted or that they will be significantly different from those proposed. The comment on section 204 is repeated here solely to provide an additional insight for the uninitiated in the workings of government. Many people naively believe that when Congress passes a law, things automatically happen. In truth, few people pay very much attention to the thousands of acts of Congress unless (a) the statute contains severe civil and criminal penalties, and (b) there is some private or political force that has interest in seeing the penalties enforced. Frequently administrative agencies will comply with acts of Congress out of fear of having subsequent budgets cut if they don't. However, this is a two-edged sword. If an administration is not in accord with a piece of legislation, noncompliance and its consequences may be the objective.

10. This standard varies widely, as noted in the text, by part of the country, time of year, weather conditions, and other factors.

11. This provision is likely to put out of business the many fine, state-licensed, independent laboratories specializing in asbestos detection. Electron microscopes are extremely expensive and rare (there are only three transmission electron microscopes in the whole state of Texas and they are used, like giant computers, around the clock).

12. The expectations of Congress did not materialize. A draft has been prepared for circulation in the Bureau and has not been released because of preliminary and unpublished determination (as of April 2, 1987) that SEM is inappropriate for measuring asbestos.

13. It is not crystal clear by what authority Congress may dictate to state governors in this fashion.

14. This plan was completed in a timely fashion and is available from EPA.

15. The 180-day deadline was found to be impossible to meet. A tentative date of October 1, 1987, was set for standards for bulk samples and October 1, 1988, for standards for air samples. These deadlines do not appear to be realistic, however, because neither project has been funded at this writing. This problem would appear to throw the entire program into great delay.

16. Twenty-three states already have legislation in respect to asbestos in

commercial buildings—Alaska, Arkansas, California, Colorado, Connecticut, Florida, Georgia, Iowa, Kansas, Louisiana, Maryland, Michigan, Missouri, Nebraska, New Hampshire, New Jersey, New York, Ohio, Oklahoma, Rhode Island, Utah, Vermont, and Washington—and 27 have such legislation as to state-owned buildings—all of the foregoing plus Kentucky, Maine, Massachusetts, and Virginia.

APPENDIX B

Synopsis of Environmental Protection Agency Proposed Rules April 1987

In late April 1987 the Environmental Protection Agency published for comment two sets of proposed rules in response to the congressional mandate contained in the Asbestos Hazard Emergency Response Act of 1986 (analyzed in great detail in Appendix A).

The first is a 230-page directive to all public and private primary and secondary schools to identify asbestos in the schools, label it prominently, and attend to abatement. The second is a 44-page "Model Accreditation Plan" for asbestos abatement contractors.

Both rules, when adopted, will have the full force of law. That is, they will have the same solemnity as if enacted directly by Congress.

Initial reaction to the proposed rules was quite mixed. As reported on the front page of the *New York Times* on April 23, 1987, Congressman James J. Florio, the chief proponent of asbestos legislation, thought the proposed standards were much too liberal while, at the other extreme, Susan Vogt, acting deputy director of the Environmental Protection Agency's Office of Toxic Substances, observed that the required standard is lower than the asbestos contained in outdoor air.

THE SCHOOL DIRECTIVE

The school directive would require schools to use specially trained persons to conduct inspections for asbestos, to develop management plans, and to design or conduct major actions to control asbestos. Schools that are subject to state laws at least as stringent as the proposed rule would be exempt from the proposed rule.

The proposed rule is preceded by an eight-section collection of explanatory material. Section I is devoted to background. It starts with a "description of the enabling legislation" — the Asbestos Hazard Emergency

Response Act—then summarizes previous asbestos activities of the Environmental Protection Agency, and then explains how the proposed rule was formulated, through the somewhat unusual procedure of what is called "regulatory negotiation." Section I also lists the members of the negotiating committee, some of whom "shared" seats. The members were the following:

1. Allen Abend, Council of Chief State School Officers

2. Bill Borwegen, Service Employees International Union and Jordan Barab, American Federation of State, County and Municipal Employees (school service employees)

3. Dr. William Brown, Baltimore City Schools, and Michael Young, New York City Law Department (big city schools)

4. Brian Christopher, Committee on Occupational Safety and Health

5. Donald Elisburg, Laborers' International Union and Laborers-AGC Education and Training Fund

6. Kellen Flannery, Council for American Private Education

7. Steve Hays, asbestos abatement engineer

8. Jesse Hill, Manufacturers of Asbestos Pipe and Block Insulation Products

9. Edward Kealy, National School Boards Association

10. Lloyd A. Kelley, Jr., Superintendent of Schools, Rutland S.W. Vermont, Supervisory Union (rural schools)

11. William Lewis, Manufacturers of asbestos surfacing products

12. Lynn MacDonald, Sheet Metal Workers International Association

13. Claudia Mansfield, American Association of School Administrators

14. Roger Morse, American Institute of Architects

15. David Ouimette, Colorado Department of Health (states with developing asbestos programs)

16. Joel Packer, National Education Association

17. Robert Percival, Environmental Defense Fund

18. Miriam Rosenberg, National PTA

19. Paul Schur, Connecticut Department of Health, and Dr. Donald Anderson, Illinois Department of Public Health (states with implemented asbestos programs)

20. Robert Sheriff, American Industrial Hygenists Association

21. David Spinazzolo, Association of Wall and Ceiling Industries (asbestos

abatement contractors)

22. Susan Vogt, U.S. E.P.A.

23. John Welch, Safe Buildings Alliance (former manufacturers of asbestos products)

24. Margaret Zaleski, National Association of State Attorneys General.

Section II contains a description in laymen's terms of the proposed Rule. Section II is set forth in full below.

Section III summarizes the alternatives considered by the negotiating committee. Section IV explains why EPA elected to use the negotiated rulemaking process. Section V summarizes the economic impact of the proposed rule. This is essentially a parroting of the analysis of economic impact recited by Congress (see Appendix A). Sections VI through VIII deal with certain rulemaking tidiness matters, such as "paperwork reduction" analysis and the like.

The following is Section II.

PROVISIONS OF THE PROPOSED RULE

A. INTRODUCTION

This unit describes the various provisions of the proposed rule. Following a discussion of applicable regulatory definitions in Unit B and general responsibilities in Unit C, inspections and reinspections, sampling and analysis, and assessment of materials are discussed in Units D, E, and F, respectively. In Unit G, the major elements of the management plan, availability of the plan, and review of the plan by Governors are discussed.

Unit H describes proposed requirements for response actions to be taken by LEAs [Local Education Administration] under circumstances described in that section. Section I explains proposed requirements for air sampling for determining when a response action has been completed.

Unit J discusses requirements to use accredited persons to inspect buildings for asbestos, develop management plans, and design or conduct response actions. Proposed requirements to protect abatement workers, custodial and maintenance staff, and building occupants are explained in Unit K.

Waivers for all or part of a State asbestos program are described in Unit L, including information required in the waiver request and the process for granting or denying such waivers. Proposed requirements for record-keeping and enforcement provisions are described in Units M and N, respectively.

B. DEFINITIONS

The negotiating committee spent much of its time crafting definitions of key concepts for the proposed regulation. Several important definitions are discussed below.

"Asbestos-containing building material (ACBM)" was proposed as a general concept encompassing surfacing ACM [Asbestos Containing Material], thermal system insulation ACM, and miscellaneous ACM in or on interior parts of the school building. These include specified exterior portions of school buildings that, for the purposes of this rule, may fairly be considered interior parts. EPA focused upon interior building materials because, in the Agency's experience, such materials represent a very large percentage of ACM in schools and appear to pose the greatest hazards to occupants. There was considerable discussion regarding other exterior asbestos materials and nonbuilding ACM inside schools, such as asbestos gloves or vehicle brake linings in garages or automotive shops, but these were not included in the definition.

The definition of "school building," in the proposed rule however, makes it clear that exterior hallways connecting buildings, porticos, and mechanical system insulation are considered to be in a building and are subject to jurisdiction under TSCA Title II. The committee believed that these exterior areas, by virtue of the accessibility of the ACM found there, warranted inclusion under the standard. Often, these exterior areas are connected to interior areas and could be considered to be a single homogeneous area in terms of a removal project design.

"Asbestos debris" is defined as pieces of ACBM that can be identified by color, texture, or fiber content as originating from adjacent ACBM. Previous Agency guidance has suggested that dust be assumed as ACM, and treated accordingly. Some committee members claimed, particularly in schools where chalk is commonly used, that dust is often not asbestos-containing and therefore areas of unidentified dust should not necessarily be subject to special cleaning practices.

"Damaged or significantly damaged thermal system insulation ACM" is defined as ACM on pipes, boilers, and other similar components and equipment where the insulation has lost its structural integrity or its covering is not intact such that it is not able to contain fibers. An accredited inspector shall classify this material based upon a determination of damage or significant damage and an accredited management planner shall recommend in writing appropriate response action.

Such damage or deterioration may be illustrated by ACM hanging from pipes; crushed, water-damaged or otherwise injured ACM; sections of ripped, torn or missing protective coverings/jackets. It may further be illustrated by occasional punctures, gouges or other signs of physical injury to ACM; occasional water damage on the protective coverings/jackets; or exposed ACM ends or joints. The definition allows that even though the insulation is marred, scratched or otherwise marked, it may not be, in the judgment of the accredited expert, damaged so as to release fibers.

EPA is interested in comments as to whether or not, in the absence of physical deterioration, the physical presence of detectable amounts of asbestos fibers or ACM powder, dust or debris from the ACM in the area is sufficient to establish such deterioration or damage.

"Damaged friable surfacing ACM" is defined as ACM which has deteriorated or sustained physical injury such that the cohesion of the material or its adhesion to the substrate is inadequate, or which, for any other reason, lacks fiber cohesion or adhesion qualities. Accredited experts will classify material based upon a determination of damage and recommend appropriate response actions.

Such damage or deterioration may be illustrated by delamination (such as the separation of ACM into layers); adhesive failure (separating of ACM from the substrate); flaking, blistering or crumbling of the ACM surface; water damage; significant or repeated water stains, scrapes, gouges, mars or other signs of physical injury on the ACM. The definition allows that such surfacing material may show signs of water damage or physical injury without, in the judgment of the accredited expert, always demonstrating a lack of fiber cohesion or adhesion.

As with thermal system insulation, EPA is interested in comments as to whether or not, in the absence of physical deterioration of asbestos fibers or ACM powder, dust or debris from the ACM in the area is sufficient to establish such deterioration or damage.

"Miscellaneous ACM" includes a wide variety of materials in buildings, such as vinyl flooring, fire-resistant gaskets and seals, and asbestos cement. Presently, damage to these materials is defined by the same cohesion and adhesion (if appropriate) properties as surfacing materials. The Agency believes this definition is sufficiently general to provide a reasonable approach to assessing damage to so wide a range of materials, although it is interested in receiving comments on this topic. Other committee members expressed interest in soliciting public comment on whether miscellaneous ACM should include non-building ACM, such as asbestos gloves or brake linings.

"Significantly damaged friable surfacing ACM" is defined as material in a functional space where the damage is extensive and severe. (The definition of significantly damaged friable miscellaneous ACM closely parallels the definition for significantly damaged surfacing ACM.) Again, this determination of significant damage will be made by accredited experts.

The definition is a function of two major factors. The first factor deals with extent, or scope, of damage across a functional space. The Agency, in draft guidance, suggested that damage evenly distributed across one-tenth of a functional space or localized over one-quarter represented significant damage (see Seventh Draft Report, "Guidance for Assessing and Managing Exposure to Asbestos in Buildings," November 7, 1986, p. 9). This represents a level of damage which a panel of experts, convened by the Agency, believed was generally, although perhaps not always, unreasonable to repair or restore.

The second factor involves the degree or severity of the damage itself. A major delamination of asbestos material, for instance, constitutes damage which is more severe than slight marks or mars. ACM, in the accredited expert's judgment, may be so severely damaged that there is no feasible means of restoring it to an undamaged condition.

Material has potential for significant damage as opposed to only potential for damage if it is accessible (i.e., subject to disturbance by school building occupants or workers in the course of the normal activities). Material within reach of students above an entrance is clearly accessible. Thermal system insulation running along the base of a wall in a boiler room is also accessible. Material on the ceiling of a school auditorium, beyond the reach of students, is not. ACM on a high school gymnasium ceiling, which might be reached with basketballs or other objects, is subject to either classification, although an LEA might be well advised in this instance to implement a preventive measure to avoid disturbance.

The negotiating committee and EPA contemplated a wide range of "preventive measures." One example is the installation of a stop to prevent a door from striking (and damaging) thermal system insulation ACM behind it. Another might involve restricting access of a corridor with surfacing ACM on a low ceiling, where students continually marred and vandalized the material. The problem of high school students hitting the gym ceiling with basketballs may be eliminated by a policy prohibiting such activities, if it can be effectively implemented. LEAs, in consultation with maintenance staff and, if desired, accredited experts, will identify a variety of creative and effective means of elimination [of] potential damage or significant damage to ACM.

If, however, such preventive measures cannot be effectively implemented, other response actions, including removal, will be required. The Act is clear that EPA, as part of its rulemaking, direct LEAs to mitigate those circumstances which involve potential for significant damage.

The "enclosure" definition requiring an airtight, impermeable, permanent barrier around ACBM to control the release of asbestos fibers into the air does not contemplate a vacuum-sealed area which is impossible to access. Instead, this definition, used in the National Institute of Building Sciences' (NIBS') "Model Guide Specifications, Asbestos Abatement in Buildings," July 18, 1986, is associated with precise engineering specifications, found in Section 09251 and elsewhere in the NIBS' Model Guide, to construct enclosures sufficiently to control fibers. Also, this term, from the standpoint of permanence, is not intended to apply to mini-enclosures described in the EPA worker protection rule or Appendix B of the proposed regulation, as these enclosures are used temporarily for repair or abatement activities.

"Functional space" is a term of art used by the accredited expert to appropriately characterize an area as containing "significantly damaged friable surfacing ACM" or "significantly damaged friable miscellaneous ACM." The "functional space" may be a room, group of rooms, or a homogeneous area, as determined appropriate by the accredited expert. Note that the functional space includes the area above a dropped ceiling.

C. LEA GENERAL RESPONSIBILITIES

The proposed rule requires LEAs to designate a person to carry out certain duties and ensure that such person receives training adequate to perform the duties.

Proposed Section 763.83 requires LEAs to ensure that: (1) inspections, reinspections, periodic surveillance and response action activities are carried out in accordance with the proposed rule; (2) custodial and maintenance employees are properly trained as required by this proposed rule; (3) workers and building occupants are informed annually about inspections, response actions, and post-response action activities including reinspections and periodic surveillance; (4) short-term workers (e.g., telephone repair workers) who may come in contact with asbestos in a school are provided information about locations of asbestos-containing building material (ACBM) and are instructed in safe work practices; (5) warning labels are posted as required by this proposed rule; and (6) management plans are available for review and that parent, teacher, and employee organizations are notified of the availability of the plan.

D. INSPECTIONS AND REINSPECTIONS

1. Inspections. Proposed Section 763.85 would require LEAs to have an accredited inspector visually inspect all areas of each school building to identify locations of all friable and non-friable suspected ACBM, deter-

mine friability by touching, and either sample the suspected ACBM or assume that suspected materials contain asbestos. The inspector must then develop an inventory of areas where samples are taken or material is assumed to contain asbestos. Finally, the accredited inspector is required to assess the physical condition of friable known or assumed ACBM as required under proposed Section 763.88.

2. Exclusions. Proposed Section 763.99 defines conditions that would exclude an LEA from all or part of the initial inspection. The accredited inspector is a key element in the exclusion process. For all inspection exclusions, areas previously identified as having friable ACM or non-friable ACM that has become friable would have to be assessed as required under proposed Section 763.88. All information regarding inspection exclusions shall be placed in the management plan.

Five types of exclusions for LEAs are discussed in the proposed rule. First, LEAs do not need to have an initial inspection conducted in specific areas of a school where ACBM has already been identified. Second, if previous sampling of a specific area of the school indicated that no ACM was present, and the sampling was done in substantial compliance with the proposed rule, the LEA does not have to perform an initial inspection of that area. Third, LEAs do not have to inspect specific areas of schools where records indicate that all ACM was removed. Fourth, LEAs can receive an inspection exclusion for schools built after October 12, 1988 (the date when management plans are to be submitted of Governors), if no ACBM was specified for use in the school. Fifth, States that receive a waiver from the inspection requirements of the rule can grant exclusions to schools that had performed inspections in substantial compliance with the rule.

3. Reinspections. Proposed Section 763.85(b) would require LEAs to have accredited inspectors conduct reinspections at least once every 3 years. The inspector must reinspect all known or assumed ACBM and shall determine by touching whether non-friable material has become friable since the last inspection. The inspector may sample any newly friable materials or continue to assume the material to be ACM. The inspector shall record changes in the material's conditions, sample locations, and the inspection date for inclusion in the management plan. In addition, the inspector must assess newly friable known or assumed ACBM, re-assess the condition of friable known or assumed ACBM, and include assessment and reassessment information in the management plan.

Proposed Section 763.85(c) states that thermal system insulation that has retained its structural integrity and that has an undamaged protective jacket or wrap is deemed non-friable.

E. SAMPLING AND ANALYSIS

1. Sampling. Proposed Section 763.86 would permit an LEA to assume that suspected ACBM is ACM. If the LEA does not assume suspected ACBM to be ACM, the LEA shall use an accredited inspector to collect bulk samples for analysis.

EPA expects that a school is likely to sample only friable suspected ACBM. For non-friable suspected ACBM, EPA anticipates most schools will assume this material contains asbestos. However, this proposed rule does not preclude a school from sampling all of its suspected ACBM, both friable and non-friable. Sampling of friable surfacing materials should follow the guidance provided in the EPA publication "Simplified Sampling Scheme for Friable Surfacing Materials" (EPA 560/5-85-030a). To determine whether an area of surfacing material contains asbestos, sufficient samples shall be taken in a statistically random manner to provide data representative of each homogeneous area being sampled.

In most cases, sampling of thermal system insulation would require an accredited inspector to take at least three randomly distributed samples per homogeneous area. The proposed rule includes three exceptions to this proposed requirement for sampling of thermal system insulation. First, an accredited inspector can determine through visual inspection that the material is non-ACM (e.g., fiberglass). Second, only one sample is required for patched homogeneous areas of thermal system insulation. Third, an accredited inspector needs to collect an appropriate number of samples to determine whether cement tees are ACM.

For friable miscellaneous material or non-friable suspected ACBM, an accredited inspector must collect bulk samples in an appropriate manner.

2. Analysis. Proposed Section 763.87 requires analysis of bulk samples by laboratories accredited by NBS. In the period before NBS has developed its accreditation program, laboratories which have received interim accreditation from EPA may be used to analyze samples. After receiving the sample results, the LEA must consider an area to contain asbestos if asbestos is present in any sample in a concentration greater than 1 percent. Compositing of samples (mixing several samples together) is prohibited.

The 1982 EPA rule "Asbestos in Schools: Identification and Notification," 40 CFR 763, Subpart F, required analysis of bulk asbestos samples by PLM and provided a protocol for analysis in its Appendix A. EPA proposes to require use of the same PLM method for this proposed rule. As it develops the accreditation process for laboratories performing analysis of bulk samples, NBS will consider whether to change the PLM protocol. If NBS recommends changes, EPA will amend this rule accordingly.

F. ASSESSMENT

Proposed Section 763.88 outlines a general assessment procedure to be conducted by an accredited inspector during each inspection or reinspection. The inspector is required to classify ACBM and suspected ACBM assumed to be ACM in the school building into broad categories appropriate for response actions. Assessment may include a variety of considerations, including the location and amount of material, its condition, accessibility, potential for disturbance, known or suspected causes of damage, or preventive measures which might eliminate the reasonable likelihood of damage. The LEA is directed to select an accredited management plan developer who, after a review of the results of the inspection and the assessment, shall recommend in writing appropriate response actions.

G. MANAGEMENT PLANS

Proposed Section 763.93 requires LEAs to develop an asbestos management plan for each school under its administrative control or direction. The plan must be developed by an accredited asbestos management planner. Some of the major components required in the plan include: a description of inspections and response actions; an assurance that accredited persons were used to conduct inspections, develop management plans, and design or conduct response actions; and a plan for reinspection and operations and maintenance.

Each LEA is required to maintain a copy of the management plan in its administrative office, and each school is required to maintain a copy of its management plan in its administrative office. These plans are to be made available for inspection by the public without cost or restriction. LEAs must notify parent, teacher, and employee organizations of the availability of management plans upon submission of the plan to the State and at least once each school year.

Proposed Section 763.93 would require local LEAs to submit their management plans to their States on or before October 12, 1988. Each LEA must begin implementation of its management plan on or before July 9, 1989, and complete implementation of the plan in a timely fashion.

H. RESPONSE ACTIONS

The proposed rule identifies five major response actions — operations and maintenance (O&M) in proposed Section 763.91 and in proposed Section 763.90, repair, encapsulation, enclosure and removal — and describes appropriate conditions under which they may be selected by the LEA. The proposed rule also identifies the steps which shall be taken to properly conduct and complete the response actions.

The LEA is required to select and implement in a timely manner the appropriate response action. Local education agencies are required to use accredited persons to design or conduct response actions. Proposed Section 763.90 specifically provides that nothing in the proposed rule shall be construed to prohibit the removal of ACBM from a school building at any time, should removal be the preferred response action of the local education agency.

Different response actions are required for each of the five major categories of damaged or potentially damaged ACBM. These categories are:

1. Damaged or significantly damaged thermal system insulation ACM.

2. Damaged friable surfacing or miscellaneous ACM.

3. Significantly damaged friable surfacing or miscellaneous ACM.

4. Friable surfacing or miscellaneous ACM, and thermal system insulation ACM which has potential for significant damage; and

5. Friable surfacing or miscellaneous ACM, thermal system insulation ACM which has potential for damage.

In each of the categories above, procedures for appropriately controlling or abating the hazards posed by the ACBM are set forth. (1) For damaged or significantly damaged thermal system insulation, the LEA must at least repair the damaged area. If it is not feasible, due to either technological factors or economic considerations, to repair the damaged material, it must be removed. Further, the LEA must maintain all thermal system insulation in an intact state and undamaged condition. (2) If damaged friable surfacing or miscellaneous ACM is present, the LEA shall encapsulate, enclose, remove, or repair the damaged area. In selecting the appropriate response action, the LEA may consider local circumstances, including occupancy and use patterns within the school building, and economic concerns, such as short- and long-term costs. (3) When friable surfacing or miscellaneous ACBM is significantly damaged, the LEA must immediately isolate the functional space and then must remove the material in the functional space, unless enclosure or encapsulation would be sufficient to contain fibers.

For 4 and 5 above, response actions for ACBM with potential for damage and potential for significant damage emphasize O&M and preventive measures to eliminate the reasonable likelihood that damage will occur. (4) When potential damage is possible, the LEA must at least implement an O&M program. (5) If there is potential for significant damage and preventive measures cannot be effectively implemented, response actions other than O&M or area isolation may be required.

Proposed Section 763.91 would require the LEA to implement an operations, maintenance and repair (O&M) program for any school building in which friable ACBM is present or assumed to be present in the building or about to become friable. The O&M program, which must be documented in the LEA management plan, consists of worker protection (summarized in Unit II.K. below), worker training, periodic surveillance, cleaning, operations and maintenance activities (also in Unit II.K.) and fiber release episodes.

The LEA shall ensure that all members of its maintenance and custodial staff receive at least 2 hours of awareness training. The LEA must also ensure that staff who conduct any activities which will disturb ACBM receive an additional 14 hours of training. Specific topics to be covered in the 2-hour and 14-hour training courses are listed.

An initial cleaning is required, which employs wet methods and is conducted at least once after completion of the inspection and before the initiation of a response action other than an O&M activity.

Proposed Section 763.91(d) would require periodic surveillance to be performed at least once every 6 months. The LEA may use unaccredited personnel such as custodians or maintenance workers to conduct surveillance activities. Periodic surveillance requires checking known or assumed ACBM to determine if the ACBM's physical condition has changed since the last inspection or surveillance. The date of the surveillance and any changes in the condition of the ACBM must be added to the management plan.

The proposed rule requires that O&M activities, other than small-scale, short-duration activities, which disturb asbestos shall be designed and conducted by persons accredited to do such work. (A discussion of what constitutes small-scale, short-duration projects is given in Appendix B to this rule.) Finally, procedures are provided for responding to fiber release episodes — the uncontrolled or unintentional disturbance of ACBM. For minor episodes (i.e., those involving 3 square or linear feet or less of ACBM), basic cleaning and containment practices for O&M staff are listed. For larger amounts, accredited personnel are required to respond.

I. COMPLETION OF RESPONSE ACTIONS

After performing a thorough visual inspection, air testing is used to determine if a response action has been completed. Clearance air monitoring will not be required for small-scale, short-duration projects. Phase Contract Microscopy (PCM) is allowed for response actions involving 260 linear or 160 square feet or less, the amounts used to trigger removal requirements under EPA's MESHAP (40 CFR Part 61, Subpart M).

The proposed rule requires the use of transmission electron microscopy

(TEM) for most removal, enclosure, and encapsulation response actions. EPA continues to believe that TEM is the method of choice for air sample analysis because, unlike PCM, TEM analysis can distinguish asbestos from other fibers and detect the small thin fibers found at abatement sites. Therefore the use of TEM will significantly improve the adequacy of cleanup and is recommended over PCM when available. However, due to limited availability of microscopes for air sample analysis and the cost and time associated with TEM analysis, the proposed rule allows a phase-in period for the TEM requirement. For 2 years after the rule becomes effective, local education agencies may choose to use PCM for response actions comprising 3,000 square or 1,000 linear feet or less. For 1 year after this, LEAs may use PCM for clearance of projects of 1,500 square or 500 linear feet or less. LEAs retain full discretion to require use of TEM at any time for any project.

The criterion for determining whether a response action is complete when using PCM will require multiple samples (minimum of five) with clearance allowed only if all of the individual samples are below the limit of quantitation of the PCM method (0.01 fibers/cm^3).

The proposed rule would require persons to use the EPA/OSHA Reference Method found in Appendix A to 40 CFR 763.121 for PCM clearance. This method is identical to the OSHA Reference Method found at Appendix A to 1929 CFR 1926.58 and very similar to the NIOSH 7400 method. (OSHA's rationale for adopting the method is found at 51 FR 22684-22692, June 20, 1986. EPA adopts OSHA's reasoning.)

The proposed rule has a three-step process for using TEM to determine successful completion of a removal response action. The first step is a careful visual inspection, as mentioned above. The two steps that follow involve a sequential evaluation of the five samples taken inside the worksite and five samples taken outside the worksite. Both sets of samples must be taken at the same time to ensure that atmospheric conditions are the same and that the comparisons are valid. The inside samples are analyzed first. If the average concentration of the inside samples does not exceed the limit of quantitation for the TEM method (discussed in detail in Appendix A of this proposed rule), then the removal is considered complete.

Stem three is taken if the average concentration of the samples taken inside the worksite are greater than the TEM limit of quantitation. In this case, an encapsulation, enclosure, or removal response action is considered complete when the average of five samples taken inside the worksite is not significantly larger than the average of five samples taken outside the worksite. A statistical comparison using the Z-Test must be used to determine whether the two averages are significantly different. (A discussion on how to compare measured levels of airborne asbestos with the Z-Test is given in Appendix A of this proposed rule.) If the concentrations are not significantly different, then the response action is considered complete. If the inside average concentration is significantly higher, recleaning is required and new air samples must be collected and evaluated after the worksite has been cleaned and reinspected.

J. USE OF ACCREDITED PERSONS

Section 206 of Title II of TSCA requires accreditation of persons who:
1. Inspect for ACM in school buildings.
2. Prepare management plans for such schools.
3. Design or conduct response actions with respect to friable ACM in such schools (other than O&M activities).

The Model Plan requires persons seeking accreditation to take an initial course, pass an examination, and participate in continuing education. Person can receive accreditation from a State that has instituted an accreditation program at least as stringent as the requirements of the Model Plan. In addition, persons in States that have not yet developed programs at least as stringent as the Model Plan can recieve accreditation by passing an EPA-approved training course and exam that are consistent with the Model Plan.

Section 206 of Title II of TSCA requires EPA to develop a Model Contractor Accreditation Plan by April 20, 1987. The plan appears as Appendix C to Subpart E. A notice issuing the plan appears elsewhere in this edition of the FEDERAL REGISTER.

K. WORKER AND OCCUPANT PROTECTION

Worker protection requirements for removal, encapsulation and/or enclosure response actions are already in effect under the EPA worker protection rule (40 CFR 763.121, et seq); and the OSHA construction standard (29 CFR Subpart G). EPA's NESHAP standard, although designed to protect outdoor air, also provides incidental protection to workers.

Essentially, under proposed Section 763.121, the regulation extend coverage of EPA's worker protection rule at 40 CFR 763.121 to maintenance and custodial personnel in schools who perform O&M activities but are not covered by OSHA's construction standard or an asbestos regulation under an OSHA approved stated plan. The EPA worker protection rule itself extended the same protections as this OSHA construction standard to asbestos abatement workers who are employees of state and local governments and who are not otherwise covered by OSHA regulation or OSHA approved state plans. This proposed rule further extends these standards to O&M workers who are LEA employees. These regulations basically establish a Permissible Exposure Limit (PEL) of 0.2 fibers per cubic centimeter (f/cm³) over an 8-hour period for abatement project workers exposed to airborne asbestos and an action level of 0.1 f/cm³ which triggers a variety of worker protection practices. These practices include air monitoring, regulated work areas, engineering and work practice controls, respiratory protection and protective clothing, hygiene facilities and practices, worker training, medical surveillance, and recordkeeping requirements.

As an alternative, however, OSHA's standard allows employers to institute the provisions of its Appendix G in the case of small-scale, short-duration projects rather than comply with the full worker protection standard. Appendix B to this proposed rule is an adaptation of OSHA's Appendix G and, thus, allows more flexibility in dealing with minor (small-scale, short-duration) projects.

None of the requirements of the OSHA standard or the EPA worker protection rule would apply if asbestos concentrations are below the action level (0.1 f/cm³). There are, however, fairly stringent requirements established by OSHA and proposed to be adopted by EPA for purposes of this rule to show that levels are below this action level for any activity, including small-scale, short-duration projects. These requirements are discussed in the following paragraphs.

Employers who have a workplace or work operation covered by the EPA worker protection rule must perform initial monitoring to determine the airborne concentrations of asbestos to which employees may be exposed. If employers can demonstrate that employee exposures are below the action level (0.1 f/cm³) by means of objective data, then initial monitoring is not required. If initial monitoring indicates that employee exposures are below the PEL, then periodic monitoring is not required.

The exemption from monitoring in paragraph (f)(2)(iii) of the worker protection rule for employers who have historical monitoring data is included in recognition of the fact that many employers have conducted or are currently conducting exposure monitoring. This exemption would prevent these employers from having to repeat monitoring activity for O&M activities that are substantially similar to previous jobs for which monitoring was conducted.

However, for purposes of this rule, EPA proposes that such monitoring data must have been obtained from projects conducted by the employer that meet the following conditions:

1. The data upon which judgments are based are scientifically sound and collected using methods that are sufficiently accurate and precise.

2. The processes and work practices in use when the historical data were obtained are essentially the same as those to be used during the job for which initial monitoring will not be performed.

3. The characteristics of the asbestos-containing material being handled when the historical data were obtained are the same as those on the job for which initial monitoring will not be performed.

4. Environmental conditions prevailing when the historical data were obtained are the same as for the job for which initial monitoring will not be performed.

When OSHA issued the final asbestos standard on June 20, 1986 (51 FR 22664), it published data from routine facility maintenance which "demonstrates a potential for exposure of maintenance personnel to concentrations exceeding 0.5 f/m^3 (fibers per cubic centimeter)." OSHA further stated:

Within the exception of wet handling, which is feasible in only very limited situations due to problems such as electrical wiring, and the use of HEPA vacuums for the clean-up of any debris generated during maintenance activities, OSHA believes that there do not appear to be any feasible engineering controls or work practices available to reduce these potential exposure to levels below the 0.2 f/cm^3 PEL and that respirators will be required to comply with the 0.2 f/cm^3 PEL.

LEAs are required, under the provisions of Section 763.91 of this proposal, to ascertain, through monitoring procedures or historic monitoring data, and to document that these levels have not been reached.

Under proposed Section 763.91, basic occupant protection requirements are established (regardless of air level) for any O&M activity in a school building which disturbs ACBM. Primarily, access must be restricted, signs posted, and air movement outside the area modified. Necessary work practices shall be implemented to contain fibers, the area shall be properly cleaned after the activity is completed, and asbestos debris must be disposed of in a proper manner.

Proposed Section 763.95 requires the LEA to attach warning labels immediately adjacent to any friable and non-friable ACBM or suspected ACBM in routine maintenance areas, such as boiler rooms, until the material is removed. They shall read, in large size or bright colors, as follows: CAUTION: ASBESTOS. HAZARDOUS. DO NOT DISTURB WITHOUT PROPER TRAINING AND EQUIPMENT.

L. WAIVER FOR STATE PROGRAMS

Proposed Section 763.98 provides a procedure to implement the statutory provision that a State can receive a waiver from some or all of the requirements of the proposed rule if the State has established and is implementing or intends to implement a program of asbestos inspection and management at least as stringent as the requirements of the proposed rule. The proposed rule requests specific information to be included in the waiver request submitted to EPA, establishes a process for reviewing waiver requests, and sets forth procedures for oversight and rescission of waivers granted to States.

Within 30 days of receiving a waiver request, EPA must determine whether the request is complete. Within 30 days after determining that a request is complete, EPA will issue in the FEDERAL REGISTER a notice that announces receipt of the request and solicit written comments from the public. Comments must be submitted within 60 days. If, during the comment period, EPA receives a written objection to the State's request or a written request for a public hearing, EPA will schedule a public hearing (as is required by TSCA Title II) to be held in the affected State after the close of the comment period. EPA will issue a notice in the FEDERAL REGISTER announcing its decision to grant or deny, in whole or in part, a request for waiver within 30 days after the close of the comment period or within 30 days following a public hearing.

M. RECORDKEEPING

Proposed Section 763.94 requires that LEA's collect and retain various records which are not part of the information submitted to the Governor in the management plan. Records required by the proposed rule include those pertaining to certain events which occur after the submission of the management plan, including: response actions and preventive measures; fiber release episodes; periodic surveillance; and various operations and maintenance activities.

N. ENFORCEMENT

The proposed rule includes civil penalties of up to $5,000 per day for violations of Title II of TSCA when an LEA fails to conduct inspections in a manner consistent with this proposed rule, knowingly submits false information to the Governor, or fails to develop a management plan in a manner consistent with this proposed rule. The proposed rule also includes civil penalties of up to $25,000 per day for violations of Title I of TSCA when a person fails or refuses to permit entry or inspection. Criminal penalties may be assessed if any violation committed by any person (including and LEA) is knowing or willful.

The proposed rule provides a process for filing complaints by citizens and requires that such complaints be investigated and responded to within a reasonable period of time consistent with the nature of the violation alleged.

Annotated Bibliography

Asbestos Action Program, Office of Pesticides and Toxic Substances. *Asbestos School Hazard Abatement Act; Report to Congress for 1985 Calendar Year.* Washington, D.C.: U.S. Environmental Protection Agency, 1986. This relatively sterile report summarizes EPA's loan and grant activity, the standards used, and the technical assistance being offered to schools.

Brodeur, Paul. *Outrageous Misconduct: The Asbestos Industry on Trial.* New York: Pantheon Press, 1985. Brodeur, an archetypal member of the class with a conspiratorial view of the world, is a prolific writer of scare books that have no substance. This volume is widely quoted.

Bureau of National Affairs. *Asbestos Abatement: Risks and Responsibilities.* Washington, D.C.: BNA, 1987. An excellent summary of state and federal laws having to do with abatement is included in this fact-filled book. It also contains a huge resource directory, case histories, financing information, certification information, and much more. Even at $75 (large discounts are available for volume purchases), this 248-page book is a valuable addition to any interested person's library.

Castleman, Barry I. *Asbestos: Medical and Legal Aspects,* Second edition. Clifton, N.J.: Prentice Hall Law and Business, 1986. This 692-page, $70 treatise provides perhaps the best available picture of the development of knowledge of asbestos disease and worker health. The author has served for many years as an expert witness and consultant in asbestos matters. In this second edition the social and industrial responses to the asbestos hazard are analyzed.

Committee on Nonoccupational Health Risks of Asbestiform Fibers, Board on Toxicology and Environmental Health Hazards, Commission on Life Sciences, National Research Council, National Academy of Sciences. *Nonoccupational Health Risks of Asbestiform Fibers.*

Washington, D.C.: National Academy Press, 1984. This 334-page work is a bit hard to read because of the many technical terms, but it provides a valuable summary of asbestiform fibers from historical and medical research standpoints. The National Academy is known for its unbiased work at the highest scholarly levels.

Cross, Frank B. "Asbestos in Schools: A Remonstrance Against Panic." *Columbia Journal of Environmental Law*, 1986. A very carefully reasoned and fully documented treatise on asbestos in schools and in buildings generally.

Dewees, Donald N. *Controlling Asbestos in Buildings — an Economic Investigation*. Washington, D.C.: Resources for the Future, 1986. This somewhat stultified book contains several economic models that would be useful in analyzing asbestos decisions from a policy perspective.

Environmental Protection Agency. *Bibliography on Asbestos in Schools*. Washington, D.C.: EPA, 1986. Contains references, frequently annotated, to several hundred government tracts, books, articles, proceedings, and reports from the 1960s to 1986.

Kline, Morris. *Mathematical Thought from Ancient to Modern Times*. New York: Oxford University Press, 1972. This marvelous treasure lives up to its title and provides insight into the relationship between the intelligent use of methematics and general human progress.

May, Timothy C. and Lewis, Richard W. "Asbestos." In *Mineral Facts and Problems*. Washington, D.C.: Bureau of Mines, U.S. Department of the Interior, 1970. Each year the federal government publishes data on commercially important minerals, their availability, their probable future use, and their alternatives. By comparing almost any substance in various years, one can glean much information about the issues of days gone by.

Ontario Royal Commission on Asbestos. *Report of the Royal Commission on Matters of Health and Safety Arising from the Use of Asbestos in Ontario*. Toronto: Queen's Printer, 1984. This tome is generally regarded as the most thorough work ever done on asbestos and it certainly is the most widely quoted by scholars and laymen alike.

Rand Corporation. *Asbestos in the Court*. Santa Monica, CA: Rand Corporation, 1985. This book is worthy of study by anyone interested in the U.S. legal system today, the "liability crisis," or related matters.

Shride, Andrew F. "Asbestos." In *United States Mineral Resources*. Washington, D.C.: U.S. Department of the Interior, 1973. See May and Lewis above.

Smith, William French, et al. *The Attorney General's Asbestos Liability Report to the Congress*. Washington, D.C.: U.S. Department of

Justice, 1981. A 232-page work that, though somewhat dated, is the best available starting point for anyone interested in the subject of manufacturers' liability for installing or making available hazardous substances.

Zelen, Melissa. "Products Liability Issues in School Asbestos Litigation." *American Journal of Law and Medicine,* 1985. This article provides an excellent summary of the legal view of the asbestos hazard. It is not as thorough as Smith et al. but affords a useful update.

Index

About
the Authors

All the photographs in this book are from a training program used by the federal government for asbestos abatement contractors and their personnel. Photographs were taken from a job site of Waste Environmental Technology, Inc. of Houston, Texas, a nationwide, leading asbestos abatement contractor.

One of the "space-suited" figures in these pictures is Carolyn Harvey, founder and president of Waste Environmental. It is no accident that she appears. Traveling almost constantly, she spends at least three days every week on job sites, making sure all is well.

Ms. Harvey's credentials as a professional environmentalist have developed over her adult life. Her interest in the subject began while studying for her bachelor of science degree in microbiology from East Tennessee State University and focused while studying for her master of science degree in environmental management from the University of Houston. Her broad professional interest has taken her from shellfish management for the Texas Department of Health, to transportation of hazardous materials for a company she founded and later sold. For twelve years, she was engaged in environmental engineering for Union Carbide, again being involved with projects ranging from control of water pollution to industrial hygiene.

She is widely published in technical circles and maintains active membership in the Water Pollution Control Federation, Texas Water Pollution Control Association, American Water Works Association, American Industrial Hygiene Association, National Asbestos Council, and Texas Hazardous Waste Management Association.

Mark Rollinson's education, interests and experience are similarly catholic. Holding degrees in economics from Duke University and in law from George Washington University, Mr. Rollinson's early career was in venture capital, having been one of the two top officers for the second venture capital institution ever listed on the New York Stock Exchange.

He has practiced law on a full-time basis for most of his career, serving for three years as Washington, D.C., resident partner for a large midwestern firm; he is a partner in the Alexandria, Virginia, firm of Smith Rollinson.

Mr. Rollinson is widely published in business, law, and topics of both specialized and general interest. While his books have been principally involved with corporate finance for smaller, technically-oriented enterprises (such as *Small Issue Industrial Revenue Bonds* and *Layman's Guide to Venture Investment Agreements*), his scholarly articles have been carried in several dozen diverse publications such as the *Harvard Business Review*, Massachusetts Institute of Technology's *Technology Review*, *Trusts and Estates*, *Armed Forces Journal*, and, most frequently, the American Bar Association's *Business Lawyer*.